SPEAKERS ARE BORN?

W S Hilton

By the same author

Building by Direct Labour 1954
Foes to Tyranny 1963
Industrial Relations in Construction 1969
The Plugdropper 1985
The Wee Spartans 1998

SPEAKERS ARE BORN?

by

W S Hilton

New Millennium

292 Kennington Road, London SE11 4LD

Copyright © 1999 W S Hilton

All rights reserved. No part of this publication may be reproduced in any form, except for the purposes of review, without prior written permission from the copyright owner.

British Library Cataloguing in Publication Data.
A catalogue record for this book is available from the British Library.

Printed and bound by Watkiss Studios Ltd.
Biggleswade, Beds.
Issued by New Millennium*
Set in 12 point Times New Roman Typeface
ISBN 1 85845 241 4
*An imprint of The Professional Authors' & Publishers' Association

Contents

Introduction v

Is Oratory Dead? 1
The Message And The Medium 7
Crumbling Cookies And Bouncing Balls 17
Setting The Tone 23
A Time To Deliver 31
Mike: Friend Or Foe? 43
Salesmen And Scientists 51
Debating To Win 59
Counsel For Committee Men 67
Meet The Media 75
Up In The Gallery` 83
Keeping Them Awake 91
Gifts From The Greeks 99
Mind And Voice In Harmony 107

Introduction

We are taught to speak almost from birth. It becomes as natural as breathing or eating. Every day we use speech in normal conversation. Yet, when asked for the first time to 'say a few words' in public, our vocal cords become paralysed and some people are almost sick with tension. One man said his fear was like going in for a serious operation without having an anaesthetic.

The lessons in this book will assist you to overcome those 'first night' nerves, for they deal directly with the reasons for them. Lack of confidence is largely because of inadequate preparation and basic speaking ability. *Speakers are Born?* helps by showing you a simple, unique and effective method of framing your speech notes, and the right presentation techniques. Other chapters outline how to deliver your speech to maximum effect.

But books have their limitations. A do-it-yourself guide on navigation, car engines or oil painting will not make you an expert navigator, mechanic or portrait painter. The theory they provide must constantly be put into practice if you want to achieve perfection.

And there is major difference between studying the usual DIY techniques and learning the art of public speaking. You can strip a car engine, or attempt your first oil painting, entirely in private. No-one need see your early, faltering efforts. Not having your mistakes exposed in public helps to generate confidence. But an audience is essential to the person who is learning to speak, right from the heart-stopping, breast-burning start.

There are a number of techniques you can learn: how to attain confidence; getting audience attention; speech delivery; how to begin and end on a 'high' note. These are all very important and this book effectively deals with them. But this is only the packaging of the speech and particularly aimed at the amateur. What about the reader who has already reached a competent speaking standard?

To progress from competence to excellence requires more than presentation skills. That is why *Speakers are Born?* includes chapters to develop the thought process: great orations of the past; logical thinking; the art of debate, and the effective use of words. Training your mind requires more time and effort than training your voice. Many people are unwilling to face the mental exertion it involves. But if your ambition is to achieve the highest level of public speaking there is no alternative; a trained voice is only of value when accompanied by a trained mind.

We owe a great debt to those distant ancestors who first struggled to communicate through the spoken word. Speech raised us well above every other primate in status and led to developments in the arts, science, philosophy and abstract thought which could never have been achieved simply through physical gestures or imitative action. The ancient Greeks realised this for they greatly valued the ability to speak well - perhaps more than any other civilisation which has followed. In the Athens of 2500 years ago rhetoric was encouraged as one of the foremost arts. In their Lyceum it was a subject in which students were proud to excel, and those who became noted orators usually emerged as leaders of the Athenian state.

Good speech is now, sadly, one of the arts that has declined in importance. The medium to convey information may have become increasingly sophisticated in the years since the last war; the message has not. Yet there never has been a time in world history when clear, considered and effective language is so essential to promote understanding between peoples and nations

In the early days of sound broadcasting there was an accepted 'BBC English' which set a good standard for the spoken word. Some radio and television programmes now appear to provide a home for the meaningless catchphrase, moronic language and cliche-laden speaker - even among the newsreaders and party politicians who appear on the screen. How can you avoid these speech defects and develop your existing speaking ability? *Speakers are Born?* has all the theory and written examples you need, but ultimate success depends entirely on the effort you put into practising them.

A final word to those who may have reached for this book to help them with their first and, perhaps, only public speaking effort. *Speakers are Born?* will do this, but I urge you to go further. Think of the many aspects of your life which a trained mind and a good level of speech would enrich: social, business and pleasure - quite apart from the personal satisfaction it would give. I hope reading this book persuades you to continue working towards that end.

W S Hilton

Is Oratory Dead?

An American survey on 'what people fear most' reported that over 40% - the largest single section – dreaded the thought of having to speak in public. Proof that this fear can be conquered is that, in Britain alone, thousands of speeches are given every week. Many from the church pulpit, even more from institutes, social organisations, local and national government. Among them a number of first, and probably only, efforts by apprehensive novices dragooned into that toast at the wedding, or tasked with presenting a gold watch to a departing colleague.

Tormented by the possibility of failure on the big day, they are envious of the practiced speaker who seems unaffected by nerves; can pour out a ten or thirty minute speech with ease and, apparently, without preparation. This convinces the novice that only he experiences the feeling of terror; heart beating like a frantic bass drum, and which has fired up and risen to lodge in his throat so he can't breathe.

He is likely to disbelieve any suggestion that the best public speakers are usually tense before a speech. But speaking in public is much like performing on the stage; actors, however experienced, are often nervous before a show. They wisely regard this as the stimulus essential to a good performance. The same is true of athletics or any other field of endeavour. The person who aims at a high level of achievement will continue to feel stress because of the increasing demand he places upon him or herself.

Yet the myth persists that top class 'speakers are born not made'. This is true only in that the speaker is certainly born, like other human beings, but without any special birthright to be a brilliant orator. His skill is acquired just like those of the butcher, baker and candle-stick maker. The incidence of birth is influential only in physical terms. A person with good stature, pleasant features and resonant voice has a head start. The unfortunates who are borne with severe facial or speech disfigurement, or badly crippled, are greatly disadvantaged. Yet there are persons who have even risen above such disabilities. None more so than the two MPs who have been Government ministers; one blind, the other deaf. There's no better example could be given that sheer willpower, effort and constant practise make the speaker, not his or her genetic inheritance.

"But I'm only going to make a single speech," complains our novice. "So have I got to read right through the book to get enough confidence for a one-off effort?"

No. The earlier chapters dealing with the structure of a speech and its delivery should get him or her reasonable well prepared – perhaps even looking forward to surprising everybody with newly acquired speaking ability. After all, you don't have to be a fully skilled motor mechanic to learn enough to change a car's plugs or carry out a simple service.

These chapters also have valuable tips for the more accomplished speaker. Surprisingly few politicians, business, or other public figures have ever taken lessons in speaking or made a special effort to study the art. Their progress has usually been empirical, gradually acquiring confidence and ability through actual experience. Frequently it shows; particularly when their upward progress to more demanding posts is unmatched by developing expertise in projecting their thoughts. This lack of basic training is one reason why even practised politicians suffer continued tension as they graduate to new and more challenging roles.

The embryonic politician will have been nervous when making his first speech to the local ward party but, if he finally becomes an MP, appearing before a party or public meeting in his constituency will not give him any sleepless nights. The dry throat and throbbing heart may, however, make an unwelcome re-appearance when he speaks to the country's most critical audience in the House of Commons. Even after years of experience speaking at constituency level, some have found the ordeal so daunting they are unwilling to face it and become almost silent back-benchers.

The one-off speaker is in a worse predicament than the emerging politician, whose faltering first effort is likely to be witnessed by only a handful of the faithful at his local party level. Their trial might be in front of a much larger number of people on an important social occasion. Their difficulty is not only to overcome the vocal paralysis which threatens, but how to prepare adequate notes for the occasion. "How am I ever going to be able to make a speech lasting as long as ten minutes?"

They are envious of those who boast the ability to get up and speak at length, without preparation, and 'at the drop of a hat'. This might seem impressive - and is usually so intended - but it is not the sign of supreme professionalism. Such speakers are seldom worth hearing. In Parliament an MP of this type is disparaged as a 'Jack of all trades'. If the Speaker is misguided enough to call one of them it usually results in a flood of business for the tea room. The good speaker knows that thorough preparation is essential - and that an 'impromptu' speech would be an insult to an audience. Churchill, our greatest orator this Century, said that every one minute of a speech cost him an hour's preparation.

The good speaker also knows that, having reached a certain level of competence, conceit should not betray him into becoming too casual in his approach to his audience, his message or its delivery. A parallel may be drawn with learner drivers. They are keen to pass the driving test so, at the start, are models of virtue on the road. The Highway Code is conscientiously studied and practised. But after passing the test many of them become arrogant about their assumed experience, and have little regard for safe or courteous driving. Instead of improving with time their driving ability actually deteriorates. The result can be dangerous for themselves and others. In public speaking such a backward step from good standards is not likely to result in the death of a member of the audience - though a delinquent speaker may bore them to that state.

Continuing the analogy: many learner drivers pay for tuition, should an ambitious speaker do the same? The question is only relevant for those who have a long term need for good spoken communication, when tuition fees would be justified. Certainly the best tuition can be helpful to a speaker at the start of his career. It should provide valuable experience of speaking in front of a sympathetic group, with learned criticism of one's efforts. Tuition is also helpful for voice production, delivery, and for widening one's vocabulary. Even so, only a small number of aspiring politicians are likely to take speaking courses. Business executives and salesmen, who want quick and effective results, are more appreciative of formal training.

Those who decide to take lessons should choose their tutors carefully, for some may be skilled in imparting a form of elocution but have little personal experience of public speaking in all its variety. Elocution lessons do have value in teaching correct pronunciation, but this is often the main objective. The form of speech taught is frequently very stylised and there may be an attempt to iron out regional accents - accents which might be of advantage to the public speaker. The elocutionary form of speech training is of more benefit to those who seek a stage career: lines from the plays of Shakespeare are often delivered in a precisely articulated but artificial manner which bears little resemblance to normal conversation.

This will not do for the public speaker. He needs to have his mind free to vary his approach according to the audience, to range over ideas and to demonstrate the originality of thought which will draw appreciation from his listeners. A speaker with these qualities will easily be forgiven less than perfect diction.

What distinguishes the average speaker from the acclaimed and envied orator? The orator can combine supremely effective language, and its controlled delivery, to make a considerable impact on his audience. Often the challenge is for him to do so on emotion charged occasions. It is the highest form of the speaker's art. Yet the confusion which exists over the true worth of oratory is shown by the entry in the Concise Oxford Dictionary, which defines the orator as one who uses "rhetoric; highly coloured presentation of facts; eloquent or exaggerating language." That description is neither accurate nor flattering, but the misconception on which it is based is shared by others - even those who write books on public speaking.

One author advises his reader to speak plainly, because oratory is almost extinct on the platform. Another is emphatic that the "amateur should not orate." This is like advising the learner driver not to enter for the Grand Prix! Each of these authors, like the Concise Oxford Dictionary, confuses oratory with the frenetic demagoguery typical of Hitler and Mussolini in their latter years.

They made their appeal to the most depraved desires and prejudices of the mob, in primitive terms suited to the lowest common denominator. True oratory, as a study of great orations through the ages will show (see chapter on `Gifts from the Greeks'), is an appeal to the intellect and made in a restrained, frequently grave, voice. If oratory is nearly extinct it is not because it is no longer effective, but because there are now few who can reach that standard of thought and delivery.

In British political and industrial history there have been renowned speakers between and during the wars; their emotionalism a reflection of the grim times in which they lived. Winston Churchill is the best-known exponent of the orator's art. His greatest efforts certainly do not fit the deprecatory description in the Oxford Dictionary, for he demonstrated that oratory is not based on frenetic speech forms, and almost always shuns them. Like the ancient Greeks his finest speeches were made at grave moments in his country's history, when the 'firebrand' approach would have been destructive of the solemn thoughts he wanted to express. And that has been true of almost every outstanding statesman down the passage of time.

True oratory is where the speaker rises above the commonplace to persuade and inspire his audience. The invaluable lesson for the student is that the greatest effect is achieved by a considered, modulated approach, using carefully chosen words of almost Biblical simplicity. All of Churchill's finest wartime speeches were like this; direct appeals to his people in language they could understand, appreciate, and to which they fervently responded. His speech during this country's most dangerous days in 1940 is a classic which repays study. For the first time in almost 900 years Britain was being threatened by invasion. But Churchill warned the Germans that if they set foot on British soil:

> "We shall fight on the beaches,
> we shall fight in the fields and the streets,
> we shall fight in the hills:
> ………..we shall never surrender."

In this speech Churchill built a rhythmic, repetitive and powerful message in the first three lines. A pause, then he growls the final hair-prickling note of defiance. During his years in Parliament, both in and out of ministerial office, Churchill made many effective and spirited speeches. But it is those solemn war time orations which will live into the future.

Churchill and other acknowledged orators were rarely seen with a sheaf of notes in their hands. Is it then the mark of the top-flight speaker that he needs no notes to guide him? That question troubles not only the amateur but also those with a fair degree of experience. Must their target be to speak well without the aid of notes? It is answered in the next chapter

The Message And The Medium

The concert pianist spends hours practising to reach and maintain his peak performance. He knows every note of a piece of music he has played, time and again, but still has the score before him on the stage. He doesn't conceal any of this, and would think it very odd if fellow musicians in the orchestra attempted to do so. Contrast this professionalism with those speakers who imply their best speeches are extempore; delivered without preparation or the need to rely on notes.

Is this just a personal conceit which does no harm to anyone? It could adversely affect the student speaker who is impressed by it, and thus given an entirely wrong impression of the task before him. Don't be misled ; the example of the proclaimed 'off the cuff' speaker is not the one to follow. (Though the phrase now usually means extempore, it originally defined the vain after-dinner performer who supposedly hid his notes by writing them on the cuff of his shirt. A casual pluck at his cuff and the next prompt word came into view!).

The speaker who boasts he can deliver a good speech without prior preparation should be regarded, at best, with scepticism. At worst, he should not be let anywhere near an audience. It may appear that a speaker has given what appears to be an excellent extempore address. But originally it was probably well researched and appropriate notes made. Having seen service on a number of occasions the outline is now firmly fixed in the speaker's mind, and he mentally edits it to suit his current audience. His expertise is the ability to do this, not to think up an entirely new speech every time he gets to his feet.

It's like the performance of a comedian. He stands up, no notes in his hand, and entertains his audience for half an hour or more. It's unlikely that any of them think his jokes were conjured up as he delivered them. They know he has his 'memory bank' into which he can reach for a selection according to whether he is performing for an all-male stag night or a mixed family gathering.

An appropriate comment on the claimed ability to speak

impromptu was made many years ago by Mark Twain, the famous American author. He was in great demand for his humorous speeches for which he was never seen with notes. After one outstanding address he was enthusiastically complimented by an admirer.

"Sure beats me," said the fan, "how you can come up with an impromptu effort as fine as that."

"Thank you," said Twain, "but I have to tell you that it usually takes me more than three weeks to prepare a good impromptu speech!"

Twain had prepared his theme thoroughly, but was able to rely on a retentive mind rather than have notes on a piece of paper. Is this the example for an aspiring speaker to follow? Certainly it is possible to speak without notes propped up on the rostrum in front of you, and with growing experience you will become less reliant on them. The ability of actors to quote large chunks of dialogue without carrying the script on stage is sometimes regarded as a role model. Admirers of the poems of Robert Burns or William Wordsworth can also recite long extracts from memory. But the art of speaking is not one of merely reciting the works of others. It is an expression of the speaker's own views on a special subject, to a particular audience, in terms they will understand and appreciate.

Preparation is the thought which goes into deciding the content of the speech, and from which he will make notes to guide him. The format of his initial notes depends on his platform expertise. They may be extensive or just a few prompt words to stimulate his memory. But whatever his use of notes the professional's preparation will be thorough, for he knows that little or no preparation is an insult to his audience. He also knows that spending adequate time thinking about the content of his address will give him a sound knowledge of the subject, that he is unlikely to be stumped at question time, and will deliver a speech which satisfies both himself and his listeners.

Careful preparation by the novice is even more essential, his notes a lifeline to which he clings for support. Under stress, his mind may falter over detail unless he has them readily available. It would certainly spoil the big event for everyone if he forgot the name of the person he is toasting (it has happened and not only to the amateur!) or the details of the exemplary work record for which, say, his workmate old Fred is getting a gold watch.

Though acknowledging the importance of note preparation, some books simply advise that "all speeches have a beginning, a middle, and an end," and speakers should plan accordingly. That is of little use to the student, for even a three word sentence has a beginning, a middle and an end. Speeches have not only three, but a number of distinct stages. The framework explained below has seven sections. These help stimulate ideas and set a clear and logical path through a speech. They comprise the 'introduction; definition; cause; effect; remedy; summary and peroration'. This unique system can be used for a ten minute presentation to old Fred, or an hour long exposition on a major topic by the professional.

The amateur will, in particular, find it invaluable in helping to overcome those platform nerves. For that tension is mainly due to lack of confidence in his subject matter; a fear that his listeners will find his message uninteresting because it is superficial or badly presented, or both. The speaker who knows he has a good story to tell is not going to be panic stricken at the thought of speaking; he is more likely to be eager to get in front of his audience. Set the various headings down and you will see how easy it is, when given the format, to build up the appropriate notes.

Introduction: The amateur may feel that, for safety, he should confine himself to an opening courtesy about his pleasure at making the toast or presentation. The professional, making a speech on , say, road accidents will have the confidence to begin with something more arresting. "Mr. Chairman, while we meet here tonight another 200 people will have been injured or killed on the roads of Britain" An introduction should always emphasise the importance of the topic for the members of the audience. People who believe they have a vested interest in the matter will listen more attentively.

Definition: Define the line you are going to take. Most topics have a number of aspects, tell your listeners which one/s you are going to deal with. An audience does not like facing the prospect of a mystery tour as a speaker rambles aimlessly around. Nor do they appreciate a speech which is so generalised as to be superficial - and sleep inducing. Once they know your message is authoritative, and targeted on particular objectives, they will happily get their minds into gear to receive it.

Cause: Here give your well marshalled facts. Not too many. Concentrate on the basic ones essential to your case, which should be precise and easy to grasp by the audience. These are at the heart of your argument; they outline the cause which gives rise to the effect you are next going to deal with.

Effect: This part of the speech outlines the benefits, or disadvantages, which result from those facts. It must be hard hitting, and convincing to your audience. If in 'cause' you gave facts showing the world's population is expanding very fast then, in this section, you drive home the effect of this on food and other natural resources.

Remedy: Here you set out your proposals to deal with the situation. If your facts were impressive, and the effects put dramatically, then your audience is more likely to support the remedies you put forward.

Summary: It is possible that some members of the audience may not remember all the important points you made. So this is where you summarise them. If the summary is done well and succinctly it will help reinforce your case, and persuade any waverer to support it.

Peroration: Now you make the final, perhaps emotional, attempt to persuade the audience to your point of view. It is the place to deploy your most effective oratory. Great care must be given to your final few words and the way you deliver them. Leave your listeners with a good appreciation of yourself, your message and its delivery.

"How is that going to help me," says the novice. "How can I use that detailed system when I'm only going to make a ten minute speech honouring old Fred?"

It will. First, write out the points you wish to make about Fred, his relationship to the company, and the record for which he is getting the presentation. Even if, previously, a mental block left you with disconcertingly few ideas, that will disappear when using the new system. In this case there's no need for the 'remedy' section; no problem to be solved.

Introduction: Thank management for making arrangements for important presentation to Fred. Proud to be selected to give speech; also apprehensive as it is first ever in public. Others might do it better but not with any greater sincerity. Pleased so many here to show Fred how much we admire him.

Definition: Fred has been good friend and colleague. Today, however, it is mainly for his service to company we pay tribute.

Cause: (The facts) Fred's been with Morton and Sons since apprenticeship days. Fifty years. Such service unique within company. Made his way upwards with ever growing skills and responsibilities. Became general foreman.

Effect: Achieved good relationship with all members of workforce and staff. Company profited by this - good staff relations are great help to productivity.

Summary: Honour a man who has been friend and guide to all. Company has benefited from his ideas on the manufacturing side. As employees we shared in benefits.

Peroration: No one deserves honour more than Fred. Wish him and his wife long and happy life in retirement. We shall miss his physical presence but his spirit will still be there to inspire us. Great pleasure personally, and on behalf of management and employees, in presenting this gold watch to Fred.

This speech will certainly – at normal public speaking speeds - take around ten minutes. Unless the novice gets carried away with his new found gift for expression and begins to expand on old Fred's virtues!

When you begin to think of the points to be included in your speech, do not stare at your notebook hoping for the ideas to come in the precise sequence you intend to use them. Waiting for the first vital sentence to spring to mind could leave you looking dejectedly at a pristine sheet of paper for some time. Jot down any point you think relevant. It doesn't matter whether it relates to the beginning, the middle, or the peroration. Get it down. Once started you will find the ideas begin to flow. And not necessarily at your desk; there are many speakers who, like authors, carry a notebook so they can note an idea wherever, and whenever, it occurs.

When you've compiled your notes, review them to decide into which part of the framework they fit. You now have the skeleton of the speech, to be fleshed out and brought alive in its presentation. The professional will bring in humorous or apparent off the cuff remarks. The amateur, unless he is particularly gifted, will cling to his original script. Before finalising the notes there is another important stage in preparation, and that is revision. A noted author once said that 'a good book is never written - it is always re-written'. It is the revising and re-drafting which results in the final, acceptable manuscript. This is equally true of a speech. So sit down with your notes and give the intended speech based on them. Speak in a slightly slower voice than you would use in normal conversation. This rehearsal will:

- Almost certainly reveal if you have your notes in the right order. As you speak through them one or two may appear to be in awkward sequence, causing you to hesitate before moving from one thought to the next. A slight adjustment is then necessary to help the speech to flow better.
- Help you to memorise the main points.
- Show the time required for its delivery. It may be too long - or you could have time to include another point or two.

In finalising your notes, aim at using simple forms of expression to convey your message. There are speakers who indulge in unnecessarily complicated words and phrases - usually intended to impress by drawing attention to their extensive vocabulary. This can make a straightforward subject appear very complex. At the end of such a speech the speaker may have confused both himself and his audience. Some of whom may think it very profound, precisely because they don't understand it! Rather like a piece of very 'modern' art which attracts the same label because few will admit they have any idea what it's about.

The words of one eminent speaker are worth constantly bearing in mind: "Any fool can use tortuous language to make a simple subject appear complex; it takes a real professional to make a complicated subject simple and understandable." This professionalism is what all speakers should aim for - but it takes considerable mental effort. 'Easy listening means hard preparatory work' just as `easy reading means hard writing'.

Excessive use of statistics is to be avoided. Piling fact upon fact may seem impressive but is more likely to bewilder the audience. A speaker has plenty of time to mull over, and absorb, the factual material he intends to use in his notes: but his listeners have to try and grasp them as they are delivered. Too many facts for them to assimilate easily and they will give up. The speaker will then have lost his audience and his case. Concentrate on the most essential statistics and get them over as simply as possible. If you don't take this trouble it is your audience who will suffer - and not always in silence.

Avoid the use of words which are highly 'coloured' or tend to exaggerate. This is typical of the flamboyant orator who may not always have too great a respect for the facts. There is no doubt that exaggeration weakens rather than strengthens an argument. Neither are 'Buzz words' or clichés impressive. (But they are so pernicious that the next chapter concentrates exclusively on the need to root them out!)

The extent to which notes are finally committed to paper depends on the speaker's ability. The best can, apparently, speak without their immediate use on the platform. But even for them there are very valid reasons for having a set of outline notes. Why?

* The salient points in a speech are determined by the time available to deliver them. Those with a particular 'hobby

horse' have far greater knowledge of their subject than can be delivered in a thirty, or even, sixty minute speech. Like the iceberg ,only a little of what they know is on show. That knowledge must be distilled until their notes provide a 'critical path' through the most powerful case they can marshall. Without this a speaker may wander from one point to another. The rest of the 'iceberg' then heaves into view as the audience gradually disappears,

* Notes help the speaker get over his case in the time agreed for his speech.

* They prevent accidental omission of important points. "I wish I had remembered to tell them" is a fairly frequent thought by speakers just as they sit down.

* Notes guarantee against a faulty memory, or time wasting deviation from the best approach to a speaker's topic. Deviation which makes him like an Atlantic sailor who attempts to do the crossing without a chart or compass, so veers all over the place. When he does finally sight land it is miles from his chosen destination. The wandering sailor inconveniences no one but himself; the wandering speaker is a trial to every member of his audience.

Notes for the novice is his insurance against stage fright, which might freeze his mind so that he forgets part of his speech. Sometimes he over-insures and has a set of notes almost equal to the complete speech. This can lead to problems in delivery for he may be so reliant on his notes that he is afraid to take his eyes from them. The result is a stammering performance as he forgets a point, retreats to his lengthy script, but is unable to find the appropriate place. Rehearsal of the speech certainly helps to overcome this problem.

Even with a full set of notes the novice may feel unsure, so he either reads from a fully written out version of the speech or tries to commit it to memory. But few amateurs have the ability to read from a script without giving a monotonous address, and stage fright is likely to make one's memory very unreliable. Actors certainly memorise before going on stage, but they have years of training which enables them to give their lines as if they were freshly minted. It is also true that some of Winston Churchill's finest orations were read in the studio from a script, but he had the expertise to make it seem as if he were speaking almost impromptu.

If you must write out your speech in full set it down as clearly as possible, in large letters, and don't have too many words on a single page. Then rehearse it until the pattern of the speech is absorbed, and this should help avoid a monotonous recital. Some speakers put each individual point on a small piece of paper or light card, numbered so they don't accidentally omit any of them. They are written or typed large enough to read without difficulty. This can be determined by placing a sample sheet at the length it is likely to be from your eyes when the notes are placed on the table or rostrum at the actual meeting.

Don't use coloured paper or ink for your notes; stark black on white is best for reading them. And don't buy a batch of coloured, see-through marking pens to illuminate what you consider specially important phrases. Some lecturers and public speakers colour their notes until they look like a modern work of art rather than a speaking script. It helps, they say, to identify the parts which need certain treatment: red for emphasis, yellow for a point which requires repetition ... and so on.

These 'traffic light' scripts do not show expertise, but reveal a speaker has not done his homework. For it is at the rehearsal stage that detailed delivery of the speech should be fixed in the mind. To rely on colour requires you to simultaneously try to read the note and decipher their mode of delivery. This leads only to confusion and a hesitant and mechanical delivery - like the music from a perforated roll fed into a pianola. Would you go out driving with a sheet of coloured notes on the dashboard telling you when to brake, accelerate, the speed you should travel at, and the route to take? Obviously not, it would be highly dangerous. The essential driving techniques have to be absorbed so you don't have to consciously think of them. You can then give all your attention to the traffic conditions around you. A speech requires the same forethought and practise. You must previously rehearse the message, and its delivery, so that you are free to concentrate on your audience.

The satisfactory speech is one in which the message and its delivery are well balanced. If your message is weak it may, to some extent, be compensated for by good speaking ability. Just as an experienced actor can triumph over a badly written script. "He hadn't much to say," observed one critic of a famous speaker, "but he said it very well!"

One of the most outstanding examples of the reverse affliction, a profound thinker but a very poor speaker, was Edmund Burke the famous 18th Century Parliamentarian. He was so boring that it drove Members out of the House when he rose to give an oration. But the next day they rushed to read in print what he had said. That Burke's thoughts live on today is proof that, in the end, it is the message which matters most.

Crumbling Cookies And Bouncing Balls

No disease spreads as fast as a cliché. An infection travels relatively slowly; a cliché with the speed of television's sound and sight. A White House spokesman in America, asked if the President intended to introduce a certain policy, replied: "not at this point in time." Within a week it became a cliché, echoed by politicians throughout the world who thought it distinguished their evasions with a certain gravitas. Into obscurity went the more direct negatives: 'No'; 'Not now'; 'Not at present'; or even the less rotund form of the original - 'Not at this time'.

Most modern clichés are simply imprecise and inelegant phrases which are intended to conceal rather than reveal the speaker's intentions. But many were once sparkling epigrams which caught and stimulated the imagination. They certainly caught the attention of many lesser speakers whose repeated, and often inappropriate, usage wore them to the point of death. Look at a list of some of those we hear every day, from TV news readers, politicians and business-men:

Agenda: Unfortunately a long-time general favourite. The only way to avoid hearing it is to switch of TV and radio - and perhaps stop speaking to the neighbours. The Oxford Dictionary defines agenda as 'a list of items to be discussed at a business meeting.' That interpretation has been widened to the point of absurdity. We now hear: 'This is not on our agenda'... 'It is part of their hidden agenda'... 'The agenda for the future'... 'I have an agenda'... 'What is your agenda?'. Convoluted and inaccurate ways of saying 'policy', 'programme', 'plan', 'purpose', 'objective' or 'intention'.

Brownie points: Why say that someone has earned 'brownie points' instead of 'approval', 'credit', 'regard', 'honour', 'prestige', or 'esteem'? Probably because it seems smarter, and shows that one is aware of the latest 'buzz' word. Usually, and paradoxically, gives the impression that the speaker is being sarcastic, rather than complimentary.

Gobsmacked: A very ugly piece of slang. Yet descended to by one Tory Party national chairman, no less, and echoed by other politicians who apparently couldn't think of 'surprised', 'astonished', 'astounded' or 'amazed'.

Ball Bounces: 'That's the way the ...' The phrase originated in America as an alternative to: 'That's hard luck...' 'that's fate'...'That's unfortunate.' For those who preferred a substitute the American's obligingly offered: 'That's the way the 'cookie crumbles'. At one time the speaking world was full of bouncing balls and crumbling cookies. These clichés have been so over-used that they are now, thankfully, nearing the point of extinction.

Track Record: People who are totally uninterested in sport, and have never seen a running track, nevertheless possess 'track records'. At election time politicians ask to be judged by the voters on their 'track records' and are attacked by opposing politicians for their poor 'track records.' But they are not the only offenders. Companies advertising even important and highly paid positions frequently ask for a 'proven track record' from applicants for a post which is definitely non-athletic. Out into limbo have gone: 'experience', 'knowledge', 'expertise', 'performance' or 'stewardship'.

If I May: Some speakers seem unable to come immediately to the point. Their remarks are prefaced with the rotund and needless: 'If I may make so bold'...'If I may venture an opinion.' They are certainly not asking permission to speak; it would be difficult to stop them. The phrase probably serves, for them, the useful purpose of giving a few extra seconds to get their thoughts in working order. But it is very tedious, and a warning to the listener that his best refuge lies in sleep.

I am Bound to say: This appears to be the opposite of the above: the speaker now implies that he is under some compulsion, not usually defined, to give forth utterance. It is just as much a forewarning of the tedium to come.

These are only a very few examples of the clichés which afflict modern speech. There are enough of them, or platitudes and specimens of jargon, to fill a book of this size. None of them bring merit to a speaker, for he is using other men's ideas as a substitute for developing his own. This can lead to a mental dullness in which clichés are repeated without any thought about their effective meaning. You should also be wary of using figures of speech which only reveal a speaker's ignorance, rather than his chic vocabulary. Many are founded on total misapprehension.

Take the curate's egg, for example. An all round Parliamentary favourite. A politician is faced with a proposal from an opponent which he knows has considerable merit. Yet outright support would mean loss of self-esteem; the implication is he should have first thought of the idea himself. Outright rejection would make him look equally foolish, so, putting on an air of gravitas, he gives qualified support to the proposal by likening it to the Curate's Egg - which was reputedly 'good in parts'. But any housewife knows there are no half-rotten eggs; they are either good or bad.

The famous curate, whose sentiment is now so frequently taken in vain, was visiting a new parishioner who offered him tea, including a boiled egg. His hostess was shocked when the egg intimated that it was very bad indeed. To help overcome her embarrassment the gallant vicar indulged in a little white lie. He assured her that 'the egg was very good in parts'.

Politicians are not the only ones who wish to appear sharp by using buzz words. Professionals in the social and scientific disciplines have their own favourites. Take the case where a little boy shows affection for his mother and antagonism to his father. The social worker, eager to categorise, glibly declares that he has an Oedipus Complex. The analogy is supposedly with the mythological King Oedipus who, the social worker believes, deliberately murdered his father so that he could marry his own mother. But this is as great a myth as the original play.

The tragedy of Oedipus, in the play by the Greek playwright Sophocles, is that he did not know the man he killed was his father or that the woman he married was his mother. His anguish, when he discovered the truth, was so great that he blinded himself by stabbing a knife in both eyes. He was, in fact, a very noble man as portrayed by Sophocles, and certainly not the undesirable who figures in the minds of those involved with children's casework.

The moral is that some clichés or slick phrases may be harmless if uninspiring, but others are dangerous because they reveal an ignorance by the speaker of his subject. Yet many of those already described may be heard frequently just by sitting in the gallery of the House of Commons. Parliament has been described as 'The Mother of Democracy.' It is also, sadly, the home of the cliché. The most senior ministers can be heard using them instead of direct replies to questions. Why? Because they are vague and ambiguous, offering no clear point on which an opposition spokesman can pursue his argument. Such ministers epitomise the qualities of a statesman as cynically described by Lloyd George; "a minister who appears to give a straightforward Parliamentary reply but which tells the opposition nothing they did not know before.

The cliché is most overworked by political leaders at a time when it should be least evident, in the 'key-note' speeches to their annual conferences. These set-pieces are intended to inspire delegates with enthusiasm for the cause, and to paint a vision of the wonderful future towards which their party is leading. But the speeches are too frequently cobbled together from general clichés and their near relative, the political platitude. The reason is that the speaker desires to draw the maximum applause from his obliging audience. And at nearly every major conference in recent years the journalists apparently arrive with stop watches to calculate the amount of applause each leader receives during his speech, and the minutes occupied by the standing ovation at the end.

But applause is often just the echo of a platitude; people will always acclaim traditional sentiments to which they or their party have subscribed over the years. Political speech writers, recognising this, tend to play down innovative ideas in speech.

For these are more likely to meet with thoughtful silence rather than the conditioned reflex which applauds the tired slogan. The platitude is also regarded as a useful device because it can be used each year - and by every party whatever its colour. Here are some of the most careworn:

* 'We are the only party which truly represents the people.'
* 'Our aim is prosperity and a better life for all.'
* 'We are for the freedom of the individual.'
* 'We are the party which stands for law and order'

The reader will be able to add others. The cliché clearly demonstrates a lack of thought and preparation by the speaker. And trying to represent a cliché-laden speech as fresh and inspiring is like attempting to pass off, as a new car, one that has been built from second-hand parts.

The use of clichés may be regarded as unfair to an audience which hopes for genuine inspiration, but the real danger is to the speaker. Relying on clichés instead of making the mental effort to find one's own apt expressions, encourages mental laziness in preparation and delivery. To be on top form, and improve performance, the muscles of the mind must be continually exercised as well as those of the mouth. So, to coin a phrase, you should avoid clichés like the plague!

Setting The Tone

The American School of Communication analysed the speaking performance of six of the country's leading politicians and its conclusion – no great surprise - was that voice approval greatly depends on tonal quality. Bottom of the poll was the state governor who not only had a reedy note, but the added handicap of 'excitable, nervous gestures'.

Women, with voices in the higher register, are at a disadvantage unless they cultivate soft, dulcet tones. When Margaret Thatcher was elected first woman Prime Minister, she was advised to make her voice less shrill and strident as it tended to alienate her listeners. Her speech projection gradually improved during the time she held office.

You don't need research to tell you about the power of an attractive vocal tone. Think of your own reaction to the speech you hear on radio and TV. The quiet, authoritative speaker is likely to enlist your support. The men who make most money doing 'voice-overs' on TV programmes or advertising features have a pleasant 'deep brown' voice. Advertisers believe it not only adds a touch of quality to their products but also generates confidence in the company producing them. High pitched, excitable voices, windmilling arms, appear rather ridiculous - which is why comedians use them to generate laughter.

It is not only the voice, but body posture and gestures which convey character. They must be calm and deliberate to show confidence and authority. No one moves fast or without an air of gravitas in the solemn and sedate royal or religious procession. To slouch, or move too quickly is to lose one's dignity in the eye of the viewer. That is why, in addition to 'funny' voices, comedians use peculiar body movements to great effect. One of John Cleese's most successful parts was as minister of funny walks.

Many politicians cultivate an aura of dignity through the use of certain body and speech mannerisms. If they look grave and statesmanlike, they reason that others will respect them at their own valuation. Playwright Bertolt Brecht made it a central theme of his famed *The Resistible Rise of Arturo Ui*, a play about the rise to power of the cheap gangster of the title, Arturo Ui. It is a biting comment on Adolf Hitler's dictatorship. Arturo Ui is a cruel and inhuman monster - the qualifications required for success in the criminal world. He gradually takes over most of the protection rackets. This is not enough for him, he also wants political eminence. But his coarse speech and slouching walk are against him.

His henchmen find a moth-eared old Shakespearean actor who teaches Ui how to walk slowly with his head up, the way to hold his hands and how to sit looking at ease. To perfect his diction he is made to recite passages from Shakespeare. Arturo Ui quickly learns how to make his voice more pleasing to the ear, to assume good posture and create the look of gravitas. He is soon on his way to further success.

Most budding speakers will agree that good posture and mannerisms are important, and can be acquired with a little effort, but protest they can do little about the voice they were born with. If we could change it at will the world would be full of wonderful opera singers. Nobody would have a voice which was harsh, discordant or unappealing.

Obviously there are limits to tonal improvement but, within those limits, most people can improve its quality. Think of the changes which occur automatically as our voices adapt to convey fear, exhilaration or sadness. The voice is also a fairly accurate health barometer. Film and stage producers use this knowledge to convey changes in the life of their characters. The man or woman originally depicted as a fit, exuberant personality is given a strong voice and upright stance. If the plot calls for that person to fall ill, this will be conveyed by a lethargic stoop and a thin, weakened voice. The voice is also used to indicate character; shrill for hysteria, whining for the untrustworthy, smooth for the conman, strong and resonant for the good and true. It is a complex instrument which can convey a considerable range of emotions depending on how well we 'play' it.

Opera singers, film and stage actors, recognise this. They spend a great deal of time and money to improve their voices. They continually practise to retain the desired level of vocal reproduction, for they are professionals and know their vocation and livelihood depend on it. Few speakers desire, or need, to give that level of professional dedication to voice quality. But it is very important to spend a reasonable amount of time on voice training. A tape recorder is a valuable asset in charting the progress of your vocal improvement. So, before you begin the exercises, make a recording of your voice. Read a paragraph from this chapter, speaking as you would normally. This is important: *unless the voice you record is your normal one - and not one put on specially for this initial recording - you will be unable to judge the improvement you achieve in tonal quality.*

Play the tape back. Listen carefully to spot any breathing weaknesses, or 'dying falls' at the end of your words or sentences. Make a note of them. One thing which will surprise and probably disappoint you - if you have not previously listened to your recorded voice - is that the taped voice is not one you instinctively recognise as your own. You may even think the thin, rather strangulated tone, with accompanying 'glottal stops', is really due to the poor quality of the recorder! We never hear our own speaking voice as others do, for it reverberates in our skull and head passages and usually sounds deeper and more resonant to us than it does to our listeners. *Now put this tape aside until you have practised the lessons in this chapter.*

Correct breathing control and good posture are important in producing the best tone. Controlled breathing is the most significant. Sound is produced by the outward passage of breath over the larynx (vocal cords). Without efficient breathing the sound will be thin - rather than full, resonant and pleasing to the listener. Breathing is an automatic function which we do even asleep or unconscious. Yet many do it badly, leading to respiratory and other problems. Shallow inhalation, and uncontrolled exhalation, are common defects. The novice's first attempt at speaking are most likely to collapse through inability to control his breathing. Taking a deep breath before you get to your feet is common, and sound, advice. But uncontrolled exhalation may see most of it expended on the first few, rushed words, leaving the remainder gabbled and indistinct.

The aim is to fill the lungs to full capacity and release your breath in a smooth, controlled manner. This avoids the need for audible gulps of air to complete a sentence. Listen to the well-trained singer; he appears to have an inexhaustible supply of air to the lungs and effortlessly achieves the most complex phrasing of the words of his song. Nor do you hear a sharp intake as he draws in more oxygen.

The average adult breathes around sixteen times a minute. After exhaling a breath the diaphragm contracts and this increases the size of the chest cavity. We then draw in a fresh supply. The amount of oxygen we need depends on whether we are at rest, shouting, singing or engaged in a hectic sport. Many people breathe so shallowly that there is little visible movement of the diaphragm - the important part of our breathing apparatus at the bottom of the rib cage. With arms folded can you feel a significant rise and fall of your diaphragm as you breathe? In engineering terms a diaphragm is a membrane of rubber or other material which acts as a pump; if it fails the pump won't work.

Correctly positioning the shoulders is a first step to rectifying any breathing deficiency. Do not, as many do, lift your shoulders as a preliminary to taking a deep breath. This creates tension and results in shallow breathing. Sit with shoulders and rib cage relaxed. Now breathe in deeply and slowly. Don't consciously stick out your chest as you do so; the aim is to expand the rib cage as a whole so you feel the air inflating the diaphragm. This will need constant practice before it becomes habitual. Air should be taken in through the nose and exhaled through the mouth. Keep your facial muscles, and especially the jaws, relaxed.

A clenched jaw is a not unusual fault in a speaker and it leads to sharp, indistinct pronunciation instead of a full, rounded effect. Your breathing should be rhythmic. Practise this by doing a count for each intake and expiration. Breathe in, 'one, two, three'. Breathe out, 'one, two, three'. Control as you breathe out is essential to producing the maximum amount of sound. The vocal length which each breath produces will differ depending on whether you are speaking quietly at a committee meeting, or faced with a large audience without benefit of loudspeaker equipment.

Check your progress in breath control. Take a deep breath

and, in a normal tone of voice, begin to read a passage from this book. Keep going until you have used all your breath and have to stop to gulp in more. Make a pencil mark at that point. Take another deep breath and this time try to control your exhalation as you read the passage. Again mark the point at which you stopped for lack of breath. You should have been able to move a little further along the page. Repeat the exercise, varying the volume at which you speak. Get your tape recorder out while doing the exercise. This will show if you are making distance without loss of voice clarity.

    Opera singers must have positive control over their breathing if their voice and tone is to sound easy and unforced. The popular ballad crooner may not need exactly the same level of technique but must still have good breath control. Play a tape by singers like Crosby, Sinatra or Como and hear the length of time they can continue without seemingly drawing in breath. (Sinatra acknowledged his 'breakthrough' was due in great part to mastering better breathing control). Test yourself. Play a song to which you know the words, take a deep breath and sing along with it. It is unlikely you can match the voice and volume of the singer without breaking off to replenish your oxygen supply. And was your intake as inaudible as theirs? This is an enjoyable exercise which should be repeated until you get near to the breath control of the singer on the tape.

    Habitually speaking through a half-open mouth, with almost no use of the 'resonators' (the nasal passages; the throat or pharynx, and the mouth cavities), gives your voice a thin, hard sound. A better tonal quality requires use of all the resonators. Many Americans speak in an attractive tone because they use their nasal passages more than we do in Britain. And some do it to excess, producing an unpleasant 'twang.'

    An illuminating exercise, for those who feel their tone of voice incapable of alteration, is to hum *through the nose*, the roof of the mouth and then down in the throat (it was said that one BBC announcer always 'hummed' himself into his best voice shortly before a broadcast. Take a deep breath and steadily exhale it in a humming sound through the nose. It will give a light resonant tone, and you should feel the vibration in the bone structure around the nose. Take another deep breath and, this time, *hum it in the mouth* - ensuring that the lips are closed and the mouth and jaws are relaxed. The sound produced will be deeper and the vibrations will be felt in the bone structure around the mouth and jaws.

Next exhale your breath while humming from *down in your throat*. The note produced should be even deeper than the other two. These exercises will prove the different, and pleasantly resonant, tones over which you have control. Practise taking deep breaths and exhaling them partly through the nose, mouth and throat – as you hum - and note the difference in tone contributed by each part of your resonators. Try these exercises while using your tape recorder. The aim is to persevere until you can hear a noticeably deeper tone while using each resonator, then concentrate on the one which gives you the best result. Your facial muscles, mouth and jaws should always be relaxed or you will not get the best possible sound - and this particularly applies to the throat.

Tension in the throat not only affects voice production, it can be painful. This often happens to the amateur because of initial fear of speaking before an audience. The voice from a tight throat passage is bound to be unpleasantly forced and hard, with little resonance. The speaker who tries to persevere with a 'throaty voice' usually ends in trouble with something resembling laryngitis. This is because the larynx, the cavity in the throat containing the vocal chords, is under continual strain. Nor is it only apprehensive novices who suffer. Some public speakers seem never to have mastered correct voice production; perhaps because they have never tried. In the last general election one of the leading politicians habitually spoke through a constricted throat. Even though he took a break from speaking engagements, he still suffered from a tired voice and had an extremely husky, indistinct tone before the end.

Practise opening the throat by first opening the mouth wide, then concentrate on widening the throat opening. The yawn is a very good exercise for this. Say 'ah', and from as low a position in the throat as possible. The sound should be deeper than usual and, after a few exercises, you will feel the throat muscles more relaxed. Keep working at it.

The final step in producing a good tone is to ensure that the relaxed face and throat muscles are complemented by correct body stance. The way you stand influences the sound that comes out of your mouth. Stand up and throw your head back as far as it will go. Try speaking now. It will be difficult to speak with the throat drawn back so tightly. Next, stand with your head bowed so that your chin touches your chest and try speaking again. The voice comes out strangulated and indistinct. Certainly the two postures are extreme and people never try to speak with their head thrust so emphatically forward or back. But many do attempt speaking with their heads at an awkward angle. Have you ever seen an opera singer with a bad, hunched stance? No, because it would be impossible to attain a full warm voice without the body also in tune.

Standing 'straight' can be difficult for some people. Tell a person who normally stands with chest stuck out, and head held back, to stand upright. They nearly always move the head forward until it almost rests on their chest and think they now look reasonably erect. But with their chest unnaturally puffed out, and their head bowed low, they are in no position for good voice production. And the person who habitually slumps, shoulders bent, will think his posture improves if he juts his head out on his neck. The result is he looks like an aggressive tortoise.

Do you stand reasonably erect? Lie flat on your back on the floor. If you can feel aching of your backbone, or other joints, it shows that you may have a normally bad posture. What we are aiming at is a confident, casual, upright stance and not the ramrod military style. The body should be reasonably erect, with head balanced on the neck, and shoulders hanging loosely at the side. The head will be on a plane in which the eyes are looking ahead almost at right angles to the body. Check that the weight of the body is forward and, like the pantomime policeman, rise gently on your toes to see if you have the correct balance. One teacher of good posture advises pupils to imagine they are suspended from a rope which is secured to a fixing at the top of their head.

Practise standing in front of a full-length mirror if you can. If it gives a front and side reflection so much the better. First hold yourself as you would normally stand, and look at what the reflection reveals. Now do the posture exercise recommended. The difference may be noticeable unless, of course, you are one of those who generally have a good stance. If you haven't, then you must repeat the exercises until a good posture becomes normal. It is not easy, and you may well forget and backslide. But good posture is not only important for good voice reproduction; it is also impressive on a platform.

The breathing, relaxation and posture exercises in this chapter, if you succeed in them, should not only improve your speech but improve your general health. When you have completed them you should be able to breathe efficiently, your voice more resonant; speak strongly and fluently and with posture improved. This is the time to get out the tape recorder again and once more record the part of the chapter you originally read before doing the exercises. Now contrast this with the first recording. The result should pleasantly surprise you, and make you much more confident of appearing before an audience.

A Time To Deliver

Preparation of your speech notes should be echoed by efficient preparation for the meeting. For example, if you leave too little time to get to the venue, your state of anxiety when you arrive will be equalled only by that of the organisers who were afraid you were not going to turn up. This won't make them feel very friendly towards you, unless you can prove that a combination of travel and other difficulties have meant you've gone through hell and high water to honour your engagement. Your audience may also be impatiently waiting and you have to go straight on without time to relax, think yourself into your speech, or chat with the chairman about his proposed agenda for the evening.

Allow ample time for the journey. If you are early, have a cup of coffee somewhere and read the day's paper and, if you can, listen to the latest news broadcast. This is particularly recommended for speakers dealing with political or other contemporary issues. One politician was widely known for his tax reforming zeal, and especially for abolishing one which particularly irked him. Before one engagement he was busy in various committees most of the day and drove to the venue just in time to go straight onto the platform. As soon as he began his favourite theme he was on automatic pilot. That was the problem.

He thundered away, like a railway train on a set track, bitterly condemning the Chancellor for failing to recognise the wisdom of his proposals. Then he suddenly sensed a slight restlessness in the audience and saw the chairman shoot him a questioning look. The reason was that the chairman, and many members of the audience, knew he was pushing hard against an open door. That evening, on the six-o-clock news, the Chancellor had announced he would shortly be making the relevant tax change!

It is courteous to the organisers to arrive at a meeting a little time before it is due to start. You can chat with the chairman and agree on the procedure for the evening; the time allowed for your speech and whether questions or discussion will be taken. You can also check on the size of the hall, and discover if you are to speak from a separate rostrum, from a table on a raised platform, or from the floor on a level with the audience. Is there a jug of water and a glass available? If the audience is expected to be a large one will you have the use of a microphone or need to project your voice more than usual (for use of the microphone see the chapter titled 'Mike: Friend or Foe?').

In some of the larger political conferences, and party press briefings, it is now fashionable for the speaker to initially sit behind the platform table but, when announced, to walk a few feet to a separate rostrum to give his speech. If so, will you carry your papers with you or see that they are neatly laid out on the rostrum ready for use? Of course, in the best of all speaking worlds you would know most of this before the night of engagement. The organisers would have sent you all the necessary information: the agenda and timetable of proceedings; a map to show how to reach the venue; whether you will be met and perhaps taken for tea; how long you are to speak; if there are to be questions and discussions, and a note about the background of the chairman/woman and any other person speaking at the meeting. Don't rely on it. Few organisers are so conscientious. You will frequently have to write and plead for this information, and still not get a reply, or merely a brief confirmation that the meeting is definitely taking place and perhaps a few relevant details. So arrive at the venue in plenty of time to check on the arrangements.

Just before you go on there may be one final, last minute, and perhaps difficult adjustment to make to the speech you have so carefully prepared. Your audience either is much larger or smaller than anticipated, Will your notes, and expected style of delivery, now be appropriate? Many speakers are apprehensive if they find they have to address a very large audience. They think it requires even more from them in the calibre of both message and performance. The truth is the opposite: a closely reasoned argument is not suited to a very large audience nor can one indulge in subtle modes of expression. There is a lower common denominator of understanding in such a gathering than in a small, interested group. Mob orators understand this. Their speeches, like that of Hitler before the dragooned audience of thousands of storm-troopers, consist of shouted political slogans. You will therefore need to simplify your message, and adopt a more oratorical tone, if you are unexpectedly confronted with a sea of faces at the meeting.

If the attendance is disappointingly smaller than expected then it would look inappropriate, and foolish, for you to be perched on a raised platform above a handful of embarrassed people. Get off the platform, sit near to them, and change your speech so that it is less formal, and allows greater time for questions and discussion. Bear in mind that your audience and the meeting organisers will probably be discomfited at the meagre attendance. Your listeners because they anticipated being relatively anonymous in a crowd but now are exposed to your full attention. The organisers because they will feel disappointed, and embarrassed at having put you to the trouble of attending for such a small audience. Adopt a manner which puts them all at ease - no matter how disappointed you may feel. And do not try to make trite consoling remarks to deal with the situation, like:

"Well, at least I'm sure we have got all the best people here tonight! You know what they say: quality is better than quantity."

It is the chairman or woman who, in their introduction, should say whatever they think appropriate and perhaps include an apology to you for the small attendance. This then gives you in your opening remarks, the opportunity to say something like:

"I thank the chairman for his generous introduction of me; it was not necessary however to apologise because there are not as many people here tonight as we anticipated. I am sure we are all disappointed about this, but I am grateful to those who have taken the trouble to attend and discuss with me this very important subject."

But let's suppose you are fortunate and your prior preparations are exactly right for the size of the meeting. The chairman has done his job well. He has settled the audience nicely in his introduction and given them a good impression of your abilities. His last few words about you will have stimulated applause and it is now time for you to begin. Don't immediately jump to your feet as if ready to tackle an obstacle course. Stand up slowly and face the audience, ready to speak as the applause dies away. Your posture should be upright but casual, your throat and face muscles relaxed. Take a deep breath and, when you begin to speak, do it in a slightly lower register than usual. This helps convey authority.

Your introductory words are vital to the success of your speech as a whole. You will lose your audience by a limpid or too tedious opening. First impressions are important. Your audience must be immediately convinced of your authority and that you are worth listening to. A track runner may get off the starting blocks badly but gradually redeem himself during the race; it is immeasurably more difficult for a speaker to overcome, in the minds of his audience, a poor, hesitant opening. So get off the starting blocks like a winner, and think of some remark which catches and maintains the interest of the audience as you go on to deliver your speech. Do not indulge in a lot of opening courtesies.

Your chairman will have welcomed everyone and remarked on any noteworthy person/s in the audience, and there should not be anything for you to add. But some speakers are unable to resist showing they know one or two local notables who happen to be present. They beam at the audience and say they are very pleased and honoured to see that so-and-so is present to hear them. Whether or not it offends the chairman it is likely to irritate at least some of the audience by the implication that they are not so important to you. Another tedious opening is to respond at length to any complimentary remarks made about you by the chairman. And even the most conceited speaker can sometimes be surprised when the chairman says how good he is! But don't get up on your feet and be drawn into a lengthy response no matter how flattered you feel. It is irksome rather than humorous to indulge in supposedly 'modest' throw-away remarks like:

"Listening to the wonderful compliment the chairman just paid me I can hardly wait to hear myself speak!" Or:

"After that enthusiastic introduction by the chairman I feel that his and the audience's expectations may be too high for my rather more modest accomplishments".

This fools no one. But it's nowhere near as bad as the approach recommended in one American book:

"The Chairman has said some wonderful things about me - all of them true. I ought to know for I wrote them myself!"

This author insisted the speaker should leave nothing to the chance introduction of a forgetful or inadequate chairman or woman. "Write your own," it strongly advised and insist that it is used. "'Then there will be no fluffing of names or dates, and you can write an introduction which will be very impressive and get the audience to accept your status even before you get on your feet."

Perhaps it works in America, but writing your own 'testimonial' is likely to get a different reaction from a British chairman/woman - and resentment that you don't trust them to do their job. They may wonder what large size of hat you normally wear! Don't attempt any of these questionable openings, for an audience has an unerring instinct for sensing false modesty and will not admire any self-preoccupation in a speaker no matter how charmingly it is presented. Such tedious remarks also intrude on the attention arresting start you should make. So, after a straightforward "Mr. Chairman (or madam chairwoman) ladies and gentlemen," go right into your introduction.

The following is an example of an opening from a speech on world nutrition to a large audience in the Midlands.

> "Mr. Chairman; during the time we shall be meeting here tonight the world's population will have grown by as many people as there are in the city of Birmingham. This fact shows that, even as we discuss ways to feed the many hungry mouths already in the world, the problem deepens. That is why, ladies and gentlemen, I am grateful for your attendance and your interest in this vital matter."

Or if you are speaking on road safety;

> "Mr. Chairman; I wonder if those present here tonight realise that, according to the statistics for deaths and injuries in Britain, they stood a chance of one in twenty of being involved in a road accident as they made their way to this meeting. And, even as we discuss this matter, many more people will be injured or killed on the roads of this country."

Should you, as an alternative, try a humorous opening? Only if you are very skilled. Audiences must have faith in the authority and sincerity of a speaker before they will relax sufficiently to allow themselves to laugh at his remarks. Comedians do it all the time, you protest, launch straight into their humorous routine and get a response. But their audiences will have gone to hear them as comedians, and they usually have considerable expertise in immediately establishing their authority and 'button-holing' the members of an audience. Your listeners will expect a serious speech, and it is only when you are effectively in control that you can indulge in a few humorous remarks which will be acceptable and welcome to them.

If you attempt an early, perhaps forced, joke it is likely to meet with silence and a growing feeling among the audience that you are lightweight and rather childish in your approach. Take, for example, an alternative opening for the speech on road safety which is intended as humorous:

> "Mr. Chairman; do you realise that every fifty seconds a man is knocked down on the roads of Great Britain ... and, ladies and gentlemen, he's getting fed up with it!"

There are a number of reasons why that could go wrong. Some of your listeners may resent jokes while you ostensibly speak on such a serious matter. The audience generally will not have become tuned to your voice and speaking pattern. A throw-away humorous remark may well be lost on them. But suppose you have shown that you are sincere about road safety, and have considerable knowledge of the subject. At that point you might then bring in almost the same remark and raise considerable laughter. For example:

> "During my speech I have had to question dubious statistics put out by some organisations involved in road transport. And we all know that statistics can be twisted to give a different slant to the problem, or may be meaningless – or almost laughable. Like the one which claims that a man is knocked down on the roads of this country every fifty seconds ... I should think he's really getting fed up with it!"

That would probably get the reaction you want because you have created a standing with your audience; you have signalled that statistics are unreliable, and you are not poking fun at accident victims but at some faceless statistician.

Whatever opening statement you decide upon, ensure that every word is pulling its weight. Until you are very experienced, and confident you can deliver the introduction word perfect from memory, write it down in large letters so you may read it easily. Having got away to a good start, don't let any bad mannerisms detract from your performance. Don't fuss with your tie or spectacles, or jingle coins in your pocket. Some speech tutors say it is because it annoys the audience. It certainly does; but the major fault is that it shows your mind is not completely devoted to your speech and that brain signals are still being given to parts of your body to twitch, jingle or fidget with your clothing. Of course these are nervous mannerisms and some say they are perhaps to be expected from the amateur, but the best way to overcome nerves is by giving yourself totally to your speech and not by distracting your own and other people's attention.

What about hand gestures? These, when done naturally, are a normal part of speech. They actually pre-date effective speech, when communication by our ancestors consisted of certain accepted hand and body signals. The deaf and dumb now 'speak' to one another with an elaborate sign language. The voice is a supremely better communicator but the tendency to use hand signals still persists. People gesture not only with their hands but also their arms and shoulders in everyday conversation. Some television presenters would be almost voiceless if their hands and arms were not meshed in top gear to their voices.

You may find that the hand gestures you use in normal conversation are suddenly difficult to repeat on a platform. Your limbs seem to have become rather stiff and your gestures are forced and ungainly, making you feel and look like a badly made marionette. Your body movements then confuse rather than clarify what you want to say. The novice should therefore keep gestures to a minimum until they become natural.

But don't put your hands in your pockets to get rid of what suddenly feel like clumsy appendages. Certainly you may have seen a number of TV commentators strolling around with their hands stuck into their pockets as if desperately trying to keep their trousers from falling down. It is a bad example; an affectation which attempts' but fails to convey a casually competent professionalism. Instead it reveals a sloppy attitude. It is unlikely that the same people would adopt a similar stance if they were speaking at a public meeting. If you are really stuck, there are three things you can do with your hands. You can stand behind your chair with your hands casually resting on the back. You can fold your arms, but not with the hands hidden like a penitent schoolboy; have them visible and pressing on the upper arms in a more professorial style. Or you can have you arms down in front of you, one hand casually holding the wrist of the other. One speaker, finding his hands a great encumbrance on the platform, was advised by a colleague to wear spectacles.

"It will make you look dignified, like a professor, as you casually put them on and off to peer at your notes then at the audience. That'll keep your hands busy."

"But I don't wear spectacles."

"No matter; get some without any lenses in them!"

The novice should not worry unduly about what seems a personal incapacity to use natural gestures. Some of the greatest film and stage performers never learned the art. The director's solution was to have them casually light a cigarette whenever they became unstuck. Look at old black and white films; nearly all the men and women in them appear to be chain smokers.

To gain and maintain authority you must appear to look directly at your audience. If you hang your head, or are constantly glancing at the walls or ceiling, you will undoubtedly give the impression of being shifty and untrustworthy. The novice finds it difficult to 'look squarely at the audience' and some speech advisers recommend searching for a friendly face among your listeners and speaking directly to him or her. It is questionable advice. In the animal kingdom, of which we are part, a stare is usually interpreted as an act of belligerence. Among Homo-sapiens only enemies and lovers look directly into each other's eyes. So anyone in the audience who was the focus of your panic-stricken stare would soon become embarrassed and unfriendly. The rest of the audience would also be turning to see why you had your gaze so firmly fixed on one particular point. Apart from the discourtesy of ignoring everyone but your unfortunate target, you can only keep control over your listeners if you keep your eyes on them. The trick is not to look fixedly at any one person but to look generally at the audience, and keep moving your head from side to side so that you appear to be encompassing everyone in what you are saying.

If your audience becomes bored how will you know this? The 'cough-meter' is a sure sign. The occasional cough is to be expected from a large gathering of people, but if it seems as if a cold epidemic has just broken out you will have lost their close attention. You need a change of tone, altered speed of expression, or greater emphasis, to try and win them back. It can be done, but it is much better not to have initially lost them. Suppose, rather than losing them, you have drawn the very intense scrutiny of some of your listeners who are so carried away by your remarks that they begin to interrupt or heckle you? Even the very best speakers are unsettled by this. Some boast that they like the cut and thrust of heckling but, if you have taken the trouble to compose a good tightly scripted speech, you don't want to be thrown off course at the whim of a hothead in the audience. Try to deal with interruptions as courteously as possible, for any sign of exasperation will please your heckler and convince him he has you on the run. That will encourage him to continue. If he seems to be sincerely trying to make a pertinent point then promise to deal with it later in your speech. Or you might say, if you need more time to think about it:

"The point about which you are concerned is a very important one. I hope that you will bring it out during question time and I promise that I shall deal with it then"

This is not running away from something that a more experienced speaker would tackle head on. Even members of Parliament, refusing to 'give way' during debate, use much the same response:

"The Hon. Member certainly has a valuable point to put and I hope he catches the Speaker's eye so that we may hear more fully about it later."

Don't believe that top speakers have the unfailing ability to 'quell the multitude' with a well chosen quip or retort. A competent speaker may deal more effectively with a troublesome heckler than the novice, but you just cannot shut up anyone who is totally determined to ruin your speech. At this point the chairman should step in. One of his main functions is to ensure a fair hearing for the speaker. If he cannot get the heckler to keep quiet he should have him thrown out. But, sadly, you may not have an experienced chairman and he simply sits and lets you deal with the matter. The only course then is to curtail your speech and ask for questions.

If the heckling still continues you are then likely to get support from the rest of the audience who object to him taking over 'their' time.

But tonight you have had an easy passage and are at the point of your peroration. It was important to start well; it is even more important to leave them with something to applaud and think about. Write your peroration to make it forceful and dramatic and have it in front of you if you are not confident of quoting it word-perfect from memory. Don't automatically assume a great peroration requires increasing volume and a higher voice note. Of one speaker it was said he started his peroration on top C and then had nowhere to go. Try, instead, the effectiveness of a pause as part of your peroration. The British seem afraid of silence. If it occurs at a cocktail party, or in conversation at the dinner table, it creates embarrassment - as if the event has been a failure because conversation has not been continuous. Yet in a speech the pause is extremely effective. (It has been said that the most difficult speaking art is standing on the stage saying nothing during a deliberate pause.) All great orators use it just before making some particularly dramatic statement. It concentrates the audience's attention on the speaker, and every ear awaits his next words. If you can attempt it reasonably successfully you will know you are well on the way to professionalism in speaking.

Try it. Just before the most important statement in the peroration, lower your voice, pause as you slowly look round the audience, then continue with the final dramatic sentence. Say it slowly, with emphasis, still looking at the audience to hold their total attention. Then sit down. Not as if desperate to gain the safety of your seat, but with dignity. Hopefully the sound of applause now enfolds you with a warm glow and you will know you have made a successful speech.

But the night is not yet ended! The sternest test may be about to come; questions and discussions are next. You had the advantage of fully preparing your speech notes, but you cannot always anticipate the questions which flow from them. This is where you either fluff it or, because of really adequate preparation, further convince the audience of your worth as a speaker. Remember the iceberg analogy. If the content of your speech is only part of your knowledge on the subject you are unlikely to be stumped by any question.

There may not be any questions. The chairman's request to the audience meets with total silence. If he is an inadequate chairman he will then smile, say that you have obviously satisfied everybody, and close the meeting. It is a poor speaker who welcomes this opportunity to dodge questions, for it is the question and answer session which reveals if he has stimulated the minds of his audience, and allows him to get on closer terms with them.

The lack of response to the invitation to ask questions does not usually signify a lack of interest, just that people are shy to take the lead. If there is not an immediate reaction from the floor, the chairman should have a friend in the audience ready to get to his feet and put a previously prepared question. Others will then almost certainly follow. Among those who do there will be some who just want to hear themselves speak; people who are genuinely seeking more information, or the irritants who wants to put some complex point to prove themselves as expert as you. Treat them all with courtesy even if one or two put their questions in an aggressive manner. Reply as succinctly and effectively as you can. If you are not sure of the complete answer don't meander on while you think of something effective to say. It will show.

Don't give another speech in answer to every question or you will soon find questions drying up and the audience will be bored - and angry. Angry because question time is their time. You have had your say and they won't appreciate you taking up most of their allocation. And don't, definitely don't, pretend you know the answer to a question when you are only 'chancing your arm.' If you have already answered most questions effectively, and the audience is applauding and seems to regard you as an oracle, it is tempting to pretend you know everything about the subject. But remember that the audience is there because they also have an interest in the subject matter of your speech. If you give a wrong answer there is a very good chance that someone will rise and correct you.

You will then lose credibility, about the veracity of your speech and all the answers you have already given. It is much better to admit you don't know the answer, and ask if any member of the audience can oblige. You will only do yourself good by this response for it shows humility, and people warm more to someone who exhibits a slight weakness than to the complete perfectionist.

In any meeting there is usually someone who asks a garbled, perhaps foolish, question. Don't be tempted to show how smart you are at his or her expense. The question may be garbled because of the nervousness of the questioner - and you ought to be able to sympathise with this. The question may also be hardly comprehensible. You should therefore try and make it look reasonable by substituting your own form of wording and then supplying the answer:

"I believe the point the questioner is making is that (here put in your clarification) and I think it is a very important point indeed. I am pleased that you have raised it. The answer is that...."

Few people in the audience will be fooled by your little ruse; they will know and appreciate that you have been kind to your questioner. He will certainly feel important because of your response and you will have made a friend rather than an enemy. Your manner will also encourage other people to put their questions, secure in the knowledge that they won't be made to look foolish. When the time comes to end the meeting the applause will be all the warmer because of your considerate response to all the questioners. And if the final vote of thanks by the chairman, or someone delegated to give it, is even more complimentary than the introduction - then you can be satisfied that you have made a good impression, that you really have delivered professionally.

Mike: Friend Or Foe?

Over 70 years ago the Bell Laboratories invented the 'electric microphone'. For the first time it enabled more sophisticated recording and broadcasting equipment. Yet the sound systems available today for speakers at meetings and dinners are frequently erratic in operation, as if the 'mike' had been invented only recently and technicians were still struggling to overcome teething problems. So the microphone, which can be an invaluable aid to good performance, is too often an infuriating hindrance.

Speech tutors warn that the mike has a delicate constitution and is easily disabled if not treated with great consideration. But you don't get the same caution in books aimed specifically at training radio and TV broadcasters. Why? Because the problem doesn't arise; it is simply accepted in professional sound studios that the equipment will function efficiently and effortlessly. And there are technicians whose sole responsibility is to ensure that it does. The equipment will also be the best available, for the quality of sound intake and output is vital to a TV or radio broadcasting organisation.

Contrast this with the systems not infrequently found in meeting halls or hotels: a tangle of trailing wires leads from a cheap amplifier to a wobbly microphone stand. The management has no technician available who fully understands the system and, if a problem does arise, may ultimately produce an employee who bears a screwdriver in hand and a bewildered look on his face. He then starts fiddling with the equipment in the hope that, fortuitously, he might rectify the fault. Hotels that would be ashamed at not producing a good meal for a dinner can be negligent about the equipment to be used for the speeches to follow.

Yet the cost of a good system, and a skilled person available to look after it, adds proportionately little to total dinner/dance expenditure. An hotel manager, looking for an excuse for the malfunctioning equipment, tends to blame poor production on the acoustics: "I'm sorry," he commiserates, "but the dining room was simply not designed to give good acoustics for speaking. You will get whistling and playback even with the very best equipment."

Then the local pop group arrives to set up its instruments for the dance after the formal part of the evening. Huge speakers are connected to them and the diners watching this are apprehensive about the prospective danger to their ear drums. Those fears are usually realised. The noise from the group is deafening; it thunders back from the ceiling and the walls. The singers bellow into their microphones, throw them about, almost swallow them - and not once is there a whistle or screeching noise to indicate stress in the equipment. It is obvious then that the acoustics are not to blame for earlier system failure, simply the attitude of the management towards buying and maintaining the best equipment.

Of course even the best system may suffer the occasional defect. A wiring connection may accidentally become loose (frequently when the top table party makes its formal entry and one of them trips over a cable!) or there is a malfunction of some part due to wear. The microphone is basically an electric ear which picks up your voice, puts it through the mixer into the amplifier and then feeds it to the loudspeakers. If even slightly damaged, the diaphragm in the mike may become insensitive. It only picks up your voice when the sound waves created are directed reproduced. There is a staccato effect with your words coming out in short bursts, as if you had a peculiar speaking problem.

Your most essential preparations for a dinner engagement should therefore include checking the loudspeaker system. Get to the venue in ample time to do this before meeting the president and other guests in the pre-dinner cocktail reception. Do not rely on the master of ceremonies doing this – though this should be an essential part of his duties that evening. Some get too engrossed in the pre-dinner formalities. And, because they rarely use the microphone themselves, tend to forget about it (MC's appear to have a rather misplaced pride in ignoring the microphone in order to demonstrate their lung power when making introductions).

You must try the equipment before the dinner starts, for it is totally unprofessional to struggle with a recalcitrant microphone while your audience waits - and not usually patiently if they've had a few drinks with their meal. In that pre-check don't simply enunciate a few numbers, 'one, two, three, four' and so on, all at the same vocal strength. Use numbers if you wish, but in the range and volume of tones you will be employing during your speech. For you have to ensure that they will all be effectively reproduced when the time comes. If you need to slightly alter the distance from mouth to microphone, to convey the full range, your testing will reveal this. If any fault emerges during this pre-dinner trial then bring it to the attention of the MC, who should have it rectified by the management. If later you are told "it is now alright" don't accept that at face value. Check once more. Alternatively, you might be told the fault cannot be corrected. Unwelcome news, but at least you will be forewarned that you must use additional vocal power to carry your unaided voice to the audience.

    The defective 'mike' can be a foe to your efforts to make a reasonable speech. A good one will be a friend in helping emphasise the quieter passages of your message by conveying the tonal qualities of your voice. There are speakers who attempt to speak at large gatherings without use of a microphone. But the greater volume to carry one's voice, the more it diminishes the possibility of effectively delivering the subdued, emotional phrasing. *The microphone should enable you to reach a large audience while speaking in much the same vocal strength as you would use in normal conversation.* Don't forget this. Many speakers do, and their voice then sounds loud and bellicose. The audience is harangued instead of given a quietly reasoned, effective, speech. The only appreciation they then have of the speaker is when at last he sits down and stops maltreating their eardrums.

    Having done your pre-check you will also know if the microphone can be adjusted for height without making a lot of protesting noise. Of course a good MC would alter it to suit each speaker as it was his or her turn to perform. If you can see this is not happening then choose the pause between the last speaker and yourself to reach over and adjust it to the level you require. Don't wait till you get on your feet then start fiddling with it. Get it right before so that you can move smoothly and effectively into your opening remarks.

At the right height and distance you should be able to use the microphone while standing comfortably and looking straight at the audience. A microphone which is too low requires you to stoop to speak into it while, at the same time, trying to raise your head to view the audience. The result is that your throat is strained, you then cannot get the vocal tone or quality you want, and you look like a rather anguished Hunchback of Notre Dame. You might think to avoid these problems by taking the microphone off its stand and holding it in your hand. Don't. After a few minutes you will feel the tension in the arm which has to keep the microphone raised to your mouth, and you will be unable to use that arm for gestures or to turn over your notes.

Your time has come and the MC introduces you to speak. Rise slowly and stand in a casual but upright position with the throat and facial muscles relaxed. Your earlier check will have shown the optimum distance from your mouth to the microphone for the best result. Take an initial deep breath and speak firmly and authoritatively into the microphone. Do not move your head from side to side, or turn away to look at the president, chairman or other guest if you include him or her in your remarks. The system only works efficiently when sound waves from your voice are directed at the diaphragm in the microphone. If they disappear, or are only faint as you move your head, your audience will be irritated by hearing only part of your speech. The trick is to be able to look round the room, while keeping your mouth as near to the microphone as possible. It is good practise to try this at home with a microphone substitute until you get it right.

Let's imagine the worst has happened just before your turn to speak; the MC or a previous speaker knocks over the microphone, or pulls out some of the wiring and there is a hasty attempt to stick it together before you go on. When you start speaking nothing is heard but a loud buzzing sound or a series of piercing whistles. You may have on occasion heard other speakers fiddling with such unreliable equipment while making jokes about its ineffectiveness. The audience may laugh but, very quickly, will become derisive if this continues. Their concentration will be broken and it will take considerable effort to get it back. It's best to put the microphone to one side and use lung power to deliver your speech.

It is possible that your mishandling of the system might be responsible for at least part of its wayward behaviour. Don't shout into it, which invites playback, and remember that some microphones are easily prompted into 'bird-whistling' if you happen to touch the thing or its stand with your hands. Of course it should not be so temperamental, but you might be unlucky on a particular engagement. In dealing with a microphone which is suspect, ensure your vocal output is smooth and the diaphragm is not subject to erratic blasts of sound waves. If you generate bird noises or screeching you should lean gently lean back from the mike until they stop. Listen carefully to any previous speaker to judge if a special approach is required to the instrument.

Faced with these problems the novice may envy the power of the MC to make announcement without electronic aid. But the MC is not making a speech, which requires the voice to deliver a range of tonal qualities; he is simply shouting an introduction or announcement at his maximum vocal strength and for only a few seconds. This would be totally inappropriate for a considered speech. Even an experienced MC would quickly become hoarse if he tried to use the same vocal output for an address lasting ten minutes or so.

What do you do if the previous speaker makes an ostentatious gesture of refusing to use the microphone? He gets to his feet and pushes it aside with all the contempt of an Olympic swimmer dismissing the aid of water wings. "I don't need that thing," he announces smugly. Resist the temptation to follow suit. It is fatuous, not professional, to ignore a speaking aid designed for your benefit and that of the audience.

No matter how well you project the unaided voice, the sound waves it produces will be heard at different strengths throughout the room. Those directly in front of the top table get it at full blast -

perhaps more than they want - while the people in the far corners of the room may have to struggle to hear everything you say. If someone at a table nearby is having a loud conversation, or crockery is rattling from the direction of the kitchen, they may simply give up trying to listen. After a few minutes of attempting to cope with all this a speaker may wish he had not subjected his voice to the strain. One thing is certain, no one will give you any kudos simply because you spoke without a microphone; the reverse is more likely.

Misuse of speaker systems is most prevalent by those who use them for street announcements. The unit may be badly mounted on the vehicle carrying it and road noises, and rattles from the vehicle, means the broadcast quality is harsh or indistinct and the message is lost. The greatest failing is that those doing the speaking are usually untrained in voice control, especially when speaking in a mobile loudspeaker unit. The speaker forgets that the system is specially designed to carry the voice, so he shouts excitedly into the microphone. The sound waves blasting out as a result will tend to exaggerate any faults in the unit, or in the voice of the speaker. Listeners in the street are subject to a harsh attack on their eardrums, and consequently alienated rather than attracted to the organisation responsible for the announcements.

The value of an efficiently used loudspeaker system is considerable - but limited. Certainly it can reach a much larger number of people than poster advertisements, and is useful for up-to-the-minute announcements about the date and time of an urgently arranged meeting, or whether a fete has been cancelled due to bad weather. But its use is questionable for lengthy political statements. Some candidates, or their representatives, are unable to resist using speakers for blaring out their message – usually unintelligibly – to the electorate. But they should remember that they have not been invited to give a talk at a particular housing estate, or to frenetically address people walking along the street. The British have a reputation for being reserved. In particular they are not pleased to publicly discuss their political affiliations or have someone else do it for them –

and at them – through a screaming loudspeaker. The prospective candidate, or his or her representatives, are always in the position of being intruders, and very unwelcome ones, if people are trying in their own homes to listen to radio, or hi-fi, or TV programmes of their own choice.

If the loud speaker must be used for this purpose the best approach is to find a suitable spot, taking in the maximum number of houses, so that the number of announcements is effectively reduced. Then ensure the speaker horn is not directed at a wall or in an enclosed space which might act as an echo chamber, thereby further aggravating those who may be listening - and taking a metal note to vote for anyone except the idiot whose name is blazoned on the offending vehicle. Stop, deliver the speech, then drive to the next point.

If you are patrolling the streets find a place to park where the vehicle does not obstruct other traffic. There are no votes to be gained from frustrated and angry car or lorry drivers, except for your opponent!

It seems a common misconception that, because a loudspeaker is 'mobile', it should be used while the vehicle is travelling. Lengthy announcements about dates, times and places of public events are given while the vehicle carrying the speaker is moving quite quickly, sometimes in a moving traffic queue. But unless the message is very simple – 'Vote for Smith' – it is unlikely anyone will hear all of it. Only the first words will be clear; the rest will be lost as the vehicle passes the listener. This only annoys those having to listen to the garbled statement; the noise assaults their ears but the message does not connect with their minds.

It is also important that the person chosen to do the speaking should be efficient at the job, and not merely whoever happens to be available and willing. Some of the most willing are frequently the most inept! Remember that using a loudspeaker is a form of broadcasting, and people listening to it will, even if subconsciously, compare it to the standard they expect from their radio or TV set. The voice should therefore be calm, reasonable and authoritative. Write out what you want to say rather than attempt to ad-lib. A pause to collect your thoughts will be more noticeable over a loudspeaker than it would on the platform.

It is a long time since 1925 and the invention of the microphone. But it remains true that care must be taken to get the best from it - to ensure it is your speaking friend and not your foe.

Salesmen And Scientists

It's autumn - conference time - and thousands of delegates are heading for the resorts where their political party, employers association or trade union is meeting. The majority will be of the silent type, interested observers, faithful reporters back to their branches but with no intention of making a speech. Among those hoping to make it to the rostrum will be the 'young Turks', burning to correct the 'deviant policies of the old fogeys on the executive' – and ambitious members for whom a conference speech provides a valuable showcase for their talents.

Both will have a far from easy time. They need to keep jumping up, arm raised among a forest of other hopefuls, in the hope of attracting the attention and favour of the chairman/woman. If they do get to the rostrum they will be firmly warned to keep to the few minutes allowed or the microphone will be switched off. That's when they begin to envy the executive committee member who is given twenty to thirty minutes to put the official line from the platform. Those 'official' speakers are in an obviously superior position. Their special status will itself command respect and attention. They are also well above floor level on a special rostrum where all can see them. Most important, they have sufficient time to develop a reasoned speech, and one which gets the close attention of delegates because it may contain important policy statements on behalf of the leadership. Nearly all cause for tension has been removed except the desire to make an impressive speech in front of their peers.

This is in sharp contrast to you, the ordinary delegate. Unknown; perhaps never previously having spoken to a large conference; having to compete to speak and, if successful, given only a few minutes to make any impact on the audience. If, almost unexpectedly, you are given the opportunity to speak you are likely to be in a very tense state. But don't rush down to the front of the hall, bound onto the rostrum, and immediately start to shout as if there was no sound equipment. Most speakers from the floor clearly hope to use their few minutes to make an impact and appear to believe that voice volume will itself guarantee the objective. So they start off shouting and end with something resembling a shriek.

The final high note, like an opera singer, almost begs for applause. There are many kind souls at conferences who are willing to oblige. Must encourage them, they reason, even for braving the terrors of the rostrum. But don't follow these futile examples and waste your few minutes faithfully repeating the crescendo approach to speaking. You will know from the earlier chapters that to conclude in a quiet, almost grave, tone of voice will make a much greater impact on the audience - even if it is only one of surprise at the innovation.

Prior preparation is crucially important for a short conference speech. On no other occasion will the time allocation be so limited that every word must be made to count. It is useless trying to deliver a comprehensive oration, the chairman will cut you off if you exceed your time. Nor will there be any sympathy from the other delegates. They also want their turn on the rostrum and if you were allowed to speak for too long - no matter how brilliantly - it reduces their chance of being called.

Make efficient use of the microphone. Start off in a calm, authoritative voice with your best tone. This in itself will catch the attention of an audience unhappily accustomed to speakers abusing the loudspeaker system thereby demonstrating their lack of expertise. Go on to deliver a carefully reasoned message. 'Reasoned' does not mean a brief compilation of pompous and supposedly erudite phrases intended to impress. Your audience will quickly see through the pretence. Simple effective phrases are best to convey your thoughts and take less speech time. Achieving this ideal is much more difficult than using the hackneyed clichés that too often suggest themselves – and which a fair number of previous speakers on the rostrum will have worked to death. Revise your speech notes and substitute plain and unambiguous words for those which, even in the slightest, smack of jargon or pomposity.

You may have only a few minutes to speak but it is enough to hammer home a well- prepared message. TV reporters are very skilled at doing this. When you next listen to the news on television note the time allowed for each news item. You will be surprised at the amount of information reporters can give, even on important world events, in just a few minutes. Of course these professionals will have had others carefully editing the material before it arrives on screen, and have a Tele-prompter to ensure they stick to the prepared script. You don't have this assistance but your objective should still be to try and make the same impact. Revise your notes, clear away any ineffectual verbiage, and this will give more time to driving home the essential points of your speech.

When you're satisfied with this basic preparation, write down your notes in lettering large enough to read while you are on the rostrum for there will certainly be no Tele-prompter to help you. Perhaps, for a few minutes concentrated effort on the rostrum, you may think it necessary to write out the speech in full. Now stand as you would at the rostrum, with notes or written script the estimated distance they are likely to be, then rehearse them in the tone and speed of voice you will use – remembering you have to do so as if speaking towards a microphone.

Continually rehearse and refine your speech until it comfortably meets the time limit which will be imposed (most conference organisers can let you know what this is likely to be). Rehearsal will also reveal if your speech is likely to sound stilted, or disjointed. If you concentrate on this task, onerous though it may be, you should finally have a concise and effective speech. It will almost certainly be better than other rostrum efforts the delegates will hear and, if that is your intention, is most likely to impress the executive. Good conference speeches have set many young hopefuls on the way to Parliament.

The major conferences are held once a year, but every week there are countless sales and other conferences in or around the major cities, and in resort hotels. Some of them cater exclusively for the smaller business end of the market, more profitable than taking in holiday-makers. During working week days they can charge twice as much for rooms as at the week end. There has been an accompanying growth in the number of organisations skilled in conference arranging. Public relations agencies are in demand for teaching the speaking techniques needed at the specialist gathering, for there can be quite a difference in speaking at a political conference and putting a message across to a sales, scientific or technological meeting. The subject matter will be more specialised and the audience comprise people who themselves have considerable knowledge of the topic under discussion.

Visual aids like flip charts, slide and overhead projectors are valuable for supplementing a speech to a smaller group. Video films are in a rather different category; they usually convey the complete message and only require initial presentation. Flip charts are the most inexpensive of aids and easy to use. But they – and the others – should be regarded like certain medical supplies, to be used only if required. Frequently the diffident speaker regards them as a kind of crutch, to give him a spurious air of professionalism. Unsure about how to efficiently use a flip chart he laboriously scrawls one word on the first sheet: 'Motivation.' This is all-important for salesmen he announces, then at length explains why he thinks so. This is worse than useless. That single written word clearly adds nothing to his vocal explanation. He has had to turn his back on the audience to write it out and so temporarily loses its attention. And the onlookers, usually fairly hard-bitten professionals, are probably surprised and not a little derisory that the speaker thought it worthwhile to use it for so simple a task. If they initially lose respect for him the rest of his talk is unlikely to make much of an impact.

A complicated equation or graph is unsuitable for use with a flip chart. Most of the listeners will be unable to absorb the statistics in the time taken for the explanatory comments.

They will still be floundering with it when the speaker has moved on. The rest of his talk is therefore likely to be unintelligible to them.

Many are attracted to the flip-chart because they can write on it as they speak. But they must be really competent to do this without losing the attention of the audience, and especially if the illustration takes some time to set out. To effectively use a flip chart its preparation should be as thorough as the main speech notes. The illustrations should be marked up before the meeting. During the vocal presentation the pages can be turned to reveal the supporting visual material without the speaker turning his back on the audience. There is an alternative to the flip chart; any statistical or graphical material can be sent out with the rest of the pre-meeting correspondence. No need to strain to read an indistinct scrawl at the meeting, the graphs or statistics can be absorbed beforehand, and the listeners can then pay attention to what the speaker is saying. The material is also personally retained for further study.

At scientific, medical or other learned conference the delegate usually has more time to prepare notes for any speech he intends to give, and has longer to deliver it. His note preparation may also be easier because he knows what the main speakers are going to say, having been circulated earlier with papers prepared by them. These papers are frequently over- scripted, even including the introductory courtesies and any jocular remarks. And too many speakers, invited to 'give' a paper, do just that. Though it is already printed and in the hands of the audience, they proceed to read it in a monotone as if the listeners were illiterate. Most members of the audience have no interest in this verbal rendition – apart from those who hadn't troubled to read the paper before going to the conference. Delegates who feel like chatting to their neighbours, reading a newspaper, or popping out of the hall for a cup of tea can do so knowing they will miss nothing of importance. The read paper is an entirely boring procedure; for the speaker and the audience, and is a waste of expensive conference time.

If you are asked to give a paper, make it plain to the organisers that it will not be a copy of the speech you will actually deliver. It will only set out the tables or other facts that support the message you want to convey. Before starting to speak tell the delegates what you intend, that you expect them to have digested your statistical material sent out with pre-conference papers, and the speech will deal more generally with your theory. The audience will then have to listen if they want to learn more about it.

Don't then be tempted to make a hybrid presentation, by frequently asking delegates to turn to one of the printed pages to look at particular tables or graphs. You may have to pause for some time before they all find them - and then even longer as they try to absorb the facts it contains. You will have lost the smooth continuity of your address, and probably most of the audience. But if you do the job well they will certainly appreciate the way in which you have tried to make your session interesting rather than a lesson in elocution. Another important consideration: you will have effectively doubled the time available for your argument by producing the written work and then using your speech to get additional information across.

At many specialist conferences the speaker will have the use of a variety of visual aids. They should not be regarded as support for those unable to effectively put across a purely verbal message. The reverse is the truth. Only the experienced can use these aids to maximum effect, moving between them and direct speech without losing grip on the audience. Before carrying flip-chart, video, or projector to a meeting the speaker must carefully consider whether any one of them is really needed to supplement direct vocal communication with the audience. Does the visual merely explain something that can be done as well, and more directly, during speech? Can the initial speech notes be modified to replace such material? Even if only a reduction in the visuals is possible it will help speaker and audience concentrate more on the spoken theme. Those visuals that are left will be the very best of the speaker's collection and command greater scrutiny.

If it is still considered necessary to use flip chart or projector don't use them to excess. The audience is not likely to be impressed by recollected images of teacher scrawling upon blackboard or using a cane to point. The tone and pace of your voice, the link between graphics and speech explanation, must maintain interest. Some insomniacs are reputedly only able to doze off when watching television, yet these programmes are produced by experts! So beware of those aids which must be used in dark, or semi-dark conditions for they can pose a particular problem. Simultaneous visual and aural concentration can be wearying to the brain. If it takes place in a darkened room some listeners may feel an almost irresistible urge to take a short nap until the lights go up again.

To counter this the speaker must be adept at matching an interesting commentary to the visual material. Some speakers appear to believe using visual aids is such a novelty that, in itself, it will maintain the attention of the audience. This is strikingly disproved by the number of people who are bored to the point of tears by their friend's holiday video. So vary the tone and pace of your voice to maintain interest, and include reasonable pauses when bringing in graphic illustrations to give the audience time to assimilate them.

Some sales lecturers appear to take the opposite view. Their talk is a combination of high pitched, urgent delivery, and a quick succession of visual slides. This can lead to an exhausted migraine for some of those who have to listen. Certainly even the best visually-aided speeches should not be too long, for the audience will simply not be able to maintain the interest level required. The wise speaker appreciates the old saying that 'the brain will only absorb so much as the seat can take'.

A final word on the growing number of European and international conferences. All the above advice applies to speaking at these events, plus two other very relevant points. The first is to understand that, when speaking to conferences where there is simultaneous translation, English is a very 'economical' language. Interpreters find it difficult to quickly translate an English speaker into German or some of the other very complicated language forms. So if you don't pace your speech a little slower than usual some of it may be lost. If the interpreters fall behind in the translation your effort begins to come through as hesitant and less effectively than you would wish. It is advisable to write out the more formal part of your speech earlier and ensure each interpreter has a copy (a good conference organiser should do this - but always check). They can then study it before you get on your feet and this helps them keep up with your delivery. Nor will there will any ambiguity about the meaning of the phrases you will be using. As you start to speak go just a little more slowly so the interpreters can get used to your accent.

The second piece of advice when speaking to an international gathering is that you must convey your ideas in easily understood words. Do not include jargon or clichés. Like some types of wine they do not travel well. The speech should be prepared so that it is comprehensible to any foreigner who has a reasonable grasp of grammatical English. If any of your phrases do not fall within that definition then cut them out. The same advice applies to jokes; attempts to put across a 'dry' English joke can fall very flat. Your audience will look at you uncomprehendingly, and you will be disconcerted at their reaction. Don't try to be an international comic.

Debating To Win

Debate is the gladiatorial arena of public speaking. The conflict is not a physical one with sword and shield. It is mental combat in which one opponent tries to prove, in front of the audience, he is intellectually superior to the other. Some are 'tub thumpers' who metaphorically take a bludgeon to the audience, hoping volume and belligerence will influence them and cow their opponents. But the skilled debater is like the fencing master with a rapier in his hand. He carefully measures his opponent, engages him to judge the speed and effectiveness of his response, then darts in with a sharp thrust whenever a weakness is exposed.

To achieve this level of expertise you must have all the skills required for effective public speaking, and an agile mind. A cool temperament is also essential because the tension is very much greater than when making a straightforward speech to an audience. (At these meetings no one has specially prepared to refute your argument, and been given ample time to do so by the chairman.) This is especially true of that most important debating forum, the House of Commons, where not one but several opposing speakers lie in wait. There the tension is aggravated because the reward for success or the penalty for failure can be considerable. Front bench spokesmen or women who lose may suffer televised humiliation, and a consequent loss of public support for them personally and for their policies. But the consistently successful will be rewarded with political advancement and their party will rise in public esteem.

At a less critical level of debate - the local party, university or literary and debating society - the outcome is certainly not so serious for the antagonists. But it will still feel like triumph or tragedy to the victor and the vanquished. Whatever the venue, pre-debate tension affects even the most accomplished. So how does one avoid finishing in the 'loser's corner'? The answer is quite simple: *you should know your opponent's case at least as well, or better, than he does.*

But is this not rather superficial advice? If debate is the

supreme test of the really competent speaker, your opponent will also have taken the trouble to research all the important facts before reaching a firm conclusion on the subject. If you both do this, and gather the same factual evidence, can there be any difference of opinion? This is an eminently reasonable conclusion but is seldom born out in actual practice. Why? There are a number of reasons. For example, many active political party members owe a very strong allegiance to no more than received ideas or perhaps family tradition. They never actively question the source evidence available. On the contrary, they may well resist any argument that shakes their beliefs because to acknowledge they have been wrong is a confession of failure to replace blind dogma with reason.

The second piece of valuable advice to the would-be debater is never be guilty of this type of mental intransigence. Seek the facts and base your conclusions only on them. An audience will be derisive of the person who is shown to be foolishly obdurate when his opponent challenges him with an undisputable fact. Being open minded to any new evidence brings credibility and stature, and helps to develop your powers of reasoning. The beliefs held by most people are usually highly subjective rather than objective, determined by financial position, their place in society or what their family expects of them. To question these beliefs might therefore be thought of as a betrayal of their friends, and traditional family values.

Not so long ago it was highly dangerous to question even fundamental dogmas. Eminent philosophers and scientists were threatened with torture, or worse, if they insisted that the earth spun on its axis or was not at the centre of the entire universe. The stake awaited anyone challenging the prevailing religious creed. So a questioning mind is therefore not a common one. That is why it is unusual to meet a speaker on the debating platform who has fully researched the facts behind his or her expressed views. If their opponent has done so he is in a very strong position. There are unlikely to be any surprises in the arguments advanced against him, and the audience will soon recognise his superior knowledge on the subject when he begins to speak. Certainly there is considerable effort involved in thorough preparation of this kind, but the reward is a calm confidence in your ability to deal with anything that is thrown at you.

Look at the likely scenario. Your adversary has put forward a case that he believes will be difficult to refute. As he forcefully delivers what he confidently considers is his final 'knock-out blow' he may glance to see if you reveal any apprehension. He is disappointed to note you look quite undisturbed. He is even more disconcerted when, as you begin your speech, you generously compliment him on his performance, then casually mention other valid points he might have made in support of his case. Your greater knowledge of the subject will be evident and you will have gained the psychological advantage – always of importance - even before starting on your own case.

Don't spend too much time doing this, or in immediately replying to all the points your opponent has put. If you do, you are letting him decide the issues under discussion. In preparing your notes you should have already considered the line he is likely to take and your speech will discount these. You can then move on to the additional facts that reinforce your conclusions. Though you may have researched a large number of facts when preparing your notes, don't risk submerging the audience in them to the extent that they fail to absorb the major points you make. Select only those that are crucial to your case and use the available time to put them over. And remember that you are trying to persuade the audience to support you, so take them through the same process of thought that led to your conclusions. You are likely to carry them with you, not least because people respond positively to the speaker who respects them as reasoning adults.

Once you have gathered all your source material, set down your notes so that one point flows logically from another. Now rehearse the argument you intend to put forward. Either speak it out loud, or go over it in your mind. Does it flow as you expected? Will the members of the audience find it as convincing as you do? Is it likely to meet the main points your opponent may make? As you rehearse, time the speech so that it approximately matches that allowed for your opening and closing remarks. Most debates consist of opening statements from both speakers, followed by each having a final speech in which one can reply or bring in additional factual material. The spin of a coin usually decides the order of speaking. Going on last is regarded as a bonus, your case being the one most prominent in the minds of the audience just before the voting.

As you rehearse your points try to consider what might be a telling counter to any of them. This not only reveals any weakness in your case but also helps you memorise all the facts. *Finally, remember that facts are important for supporting your views, but debates are not about facts but about opinion or principles.* Facts cannot be debated. A fact is the truth of any matter or, as the logician would say: 'a fact is the thing that is'.

Yet many people say something like: 'that is an untrue fact'. It is as ludicrous as saying: 'that is not the true truth.' So if your opponent starts to argue on what is known to be a point of fact – though apparently not to him - correct him when it is your turn to speak. It is critical that one does not waste time debating a matter of fact as against a matter of principle. As an analogy think of the type of debate that frequently happens in the workplace or the pub. Two men might argue all night about whether a cup winning football team of ten years ago comprised certain players. Yet this is a fact which can be established simply by looking up the records. But suppose their disagreement is about whether Jones was a better player than Smith. This is a matter of judgement which can be debated. The facts are then brought in to support the conclusions; the number of times either played for their national teams, the goals scored during their playing career, or the eminent clubs competing to sign them.

Your opponent in a debate may, of course, deny that your case is founded on hard facts. He will then be relying on the audience being unsure as to who is telling the truth. So where the main points of your case involve citing public, or other available statistics, take the relevant publication with you as a back up, or details of where the fact/s may be found. One Member of Parliament was known for his debating skills and, through the years, he had learned all the tricks of this particular trade. The major points, where he thought his opponent might challenge him, were marked up in the relevant publications. He would, if challenged, simply reach for the relevant document. For maximum effect he never read the passage himself, anticipating that his hard-pressed opponent might simply bluster that he had misquoted. He handed it to the chairman of the meeting and asked him to read it out. After this his opponent was well on the way to losing the confidence of his audience.

On one occasion his opponent raised some obscure 'fact' which he insisted was crucial to the success of his case, and destructive of the MP's view. The politician had not prepared for this but thought he knew the truth of the point at issue, and that his adversary was either misguided or mendacious. How could this be effectively demonstrated to the audience? He forced the issue by quoting his own version and added: "If I cannot send the chairman support for my view within seven days of this meeting I will donate £50 to the local hospital charity. Will my opponent do the same?"

The opposing speaker looked embarrassed for a moment, then muttered that he didn't gamble. But he had - and lost. For his response failed to convince the audience. Some speakers try to gain credence for such supposed 'facts' by insisting that "everyone knows they are true" or that they have heard them from well-known people. It is a dubious tactic, audiences are not complimented when told they should favour an argument simply because someone else did. They want to be respected as people able to make up their own minds. So the way to win their confidence, and the debate, is to present properly marshalled facts to support your conclusions and upon which you invite their judgement.

But the speaker with the best case does not always win the verdict! Especially if he is a less accomplished performer than his opponent. Audiences do not comprise high court judges skilled in distinguishing fact from rhetoric or showmanship. They support a speaker not only on his message, but on the way he puts it over, his dress, mannerisms and personality. So you may find yourself facing an opponent who, whatever he lacks in mental application or soundness of argument, is very skilled and persuasive. Some even dress to intimidate and consciously affect mannerisms intended to imply that they have a superior intellect. They may have a shaggy mane of hair which is carried down their face to end in a 'philosopher's beard'. When speaking their eyes tend to look towards the ceiling as if for inspiration. The whole image suggests the intellectually brilliant but absent minded professor who is so pre-occupied, and deep in thought, that he is disinterested in the more mundane things in life like clothes and general appearance.

His opponent, if impressed by all of this, will be at a psychological disadvantage even before the debate starts. That is the effect the hirsute one intends. Take comfort from the words of the old Greek proverb (when such posturing was evident in the schools of rhetoric) that: 'The beard does not make the philosopher'. Nor does such 'dressing for the occasion' signal the possession of a powerful intellect; usually the opposite. A man who is confident in his intellectual ability does not need to supplement it by the protective armour of the beard or unusual dress. And your best armour against the poseur is knowing the facts and having rehearsed them until they are embedded in your mind.

Some debaters try to be witty, or sarcastic, at the expense of opposing speakers. The objective is to make them lose their temper. There is strong temptation to respond in kind, especially if the audience appears to find the remarks amusing. But don't be drawn into retaliation, and don't make the mistake of thinking audiences are impressed - even if they do laugh - by smart or snide repartee. Be courteous to your opponent whatever his attitude to you. To lose your temper means you are on the way to losing the argument. In the Far East a loss of temper is, rightly, looked upon as a 'loss of face.' So try to convey no visible emotion which might give satisfaction to your opponent. To show no sign of being concerned by his remarks will certainly help to unsettle him. Apart from this it must be firmly remembered that a loss of emotional control will inhibit your ability to think logically. If your opponent is particularly offensive, or makes a number of personal remarks, you can deal with this in two ways. The first is just to ignore them completely. The second is to say something which is a cool 'put down' like:

"My opponent has made a number of remarks about me, and I am flattered by his considerable personal interest. But I am sure those listening do not wish to hear further details of my life story, or of his. I hope he will not find me ungracious if, instead, I confine my remarks to the facts of my case which I hope will find support with the members of the audience."

Another valid reason why you should never indulge in personalities is that it is, in every sense, a waste of time. It gains you no friends, and takes up time that is much better spent on setting out your speech. And time is of the essence in a debate. Each speaker is usually given a set number of minutes in which to make his opening statement and concluding speech. To over-run the time allowed incurs the displeasure of the chairman and you will look completely amateurish to the audience if, in consequence, he has to put you down. They might also suspect you of 'gamesmanship' by trying to steal a few more minutes for your speech than you have been allowed.

So keep an eye on the clock, if there is one visible in the hall, to make sure you conclude your first period on time. If there isn't one, put your watch on the table where you can clearly see it. How do you pace your speech so that you neither take less or more time than allowed? It is certainly not advisable to compile a finalised set of notes that are intended to fill the exact time allotted to you; no more, no less. For during the debate you may speak a little faster than usual, in response to an encouraging reaction from the audience, or you may decide to give a little more time to one particular aspect which the audience appears to favour. The competent speaker will have prepared for these eventualities. His notes will include more material than he thinks necessary, but certain items will be earmarked as those which can be expanded or jettisoned to fit the time at his disposal.

In your first speaking period you had the advantage of detailed preparation of your case and the order in which you intended to put it forward. But the most testing time comes when each speaker has the second session to reply to his opponent's arguments. It is this stage of the debate that reveals the inferiority of the person who has not prepared thoroughly. He is disconcerted by any facts brought out by his opponent which he had either not considered, or were unknown to him. His only recourse is to ignore them and hope the audience will have done the same. This, of course, will not happen to you! You have done all your research and, above all, know your opponent's case better than he does. He cannot mention anything that is new or unsettling for you. In your reply you are effortlessly able to deal with any of his arguments and still have a great deal in reserve.

End your speech in the same manner as you delivered it, with courtesy to the audience, your opponent and the chairman. Do not, however, simply content yourself with these civilities for a rather tame ending. Leave enough time for them and a brief reiteration of the reasons for asking the audience to support your conclusions. Say something like:

"At this point I would like to express my thanks to the audience for their kind attention, my opponent for the fair and courteous way in which he put his case and you, Mr. Chairman, for the excellent manner in which you have conducted the meeting. I hope the audience will support the views I have put forward tonight. I do so in the very firm belief that ..."

You now briefly summarise the facts expounded in your speech, thus reminding your audience of them. Leave the most important point to the last as the basis for your short peroration. Suppose your opponent is, unusually, as well prepared for the debate as you are. The audience will then be in for a remarkable evening!

Counsel For Committee Men

A venerable British tradition is that when decisions have to be made two heads are better than one. But too many heads and you might never get a decision made – or it can take a long, frustrating time. The solution? The parent organisation sets up a committee to do the work. The choice is wide: regular, standing, joint or ad-hoc among them. They all carry out some special function and can be found in organisations ranging from the Women's Institute, Rotary, trade union, employers association, board of directors, to the Houses of Parliament.

Whatever their name, committees all have one main feature in common; they are given special duties and powers on behalf of the organisation which creates them. Usually the more experienced members are elected to sit on the most important or, if there are few willing to serve, those who can be cajoled or brow-beaten into taking office. For the budding speaker any proffered committee membership should be seized with both hands. There is no better training ground, no opportunity more valuable for gradually developing speaking and debating skills – and at your own pace because:

- They meet more often than the main councils that set them up.
- With a limited membership so there is less competition to catch the chairman's attention and to take part in discussion.
- Have smaller numbers on the committee so speaking to them is less tense for the amateur.

The beginner need only say a few words at first, then move on to making longer speeches as his confidence and ability grows. And becoming familiar with the meeting papers and procedure, makes for confidence when speaking before the larger main council sessions.

Many organisations provide the possibility of progressive development. The ambitious speaker can, by proving himself, climb from the local branch committee, through district or regional level, right to the national executive. At each stage he will have the opportunity of discussion with colleagues who have wider experience. Learning from them will be invaluable in improving his own abilities, providing he is willing to listen. Willingness to listen to words of greater wisdom than your own is, however not particularly widespread. But 'to learn you must first listen' should be the maxim of the person who wants to advance his abilities as quickly as possible.

Acceptance of committee membership implies that you will play a constructive part in its work and attend as many meetings as possible. Do not follow the example of the hardened cynic – at least one on every committee - who seems to have no other reason for being on committee except to disrupt its work, and whose apparent philosophy is:

1. Seldom come to meetings but if you do, come late.
2. If the weather is a little doubtful, don't think of coming.
3 Never read the relevant committee papers till the last minute.
4. Always find fault with the officers but never accept office.
5. It is much easier to destructively criticise than do anything constructive.
6. If you are not appointed to an important sub-committee be upset.
7. If you are nominated, only accept reluctantly. Rules 1 to 3 above then apply.
8. If asked by the chairman to give an opinion, decline to do so.
9. After the meeting tell the chairman what the decision should have been.
10. Avoid doing anything to further the committee's work.
11. When others do the work accuse them of running the committee by clique.

If you as a new committee member do exactly the opposite of this, it won't be long before you are respected as a valuable member of the committee, with the more mature and constructive members pleased to help and encourage your development.

You should carefully study your committee's agenda and relevant papers as soon as you get them. This gives you maximum time to research your facts before the meeting if you want to speak on any matter. Superficial advice? On the contrary, few members of any committee or council do this. It is regular practice for some to read them on the way to the meeting, or in the room just before it starts. So even though you are a new committee member you will, by prior study of the papers, be more knowledgeable about the business than many of your committee colleagues.

As you intend to take part in discussion as often as possible so you must first know and understand the standing orders applying to the conduct of meetings. These procedural rules will govern what you can, and cannot do, during debate. A committee without standing orders would be like a ship without a rudder. Standing orders define such matters as procedure; election of officers and any subsidiary committee; number and starting times of meetings; length of speeches, and the manner in which motions and amendments may be put. Unlike the constitution of the organisation, which can only be changed at annual meetings, standing orders can be suspended at any time should it be considered essential.

For example; the committee may have taken a decision at one meeting then find, at the next, new information makes it important it should be urgently reversed. But the standing orders of most organisations contain a clause that any matter which has been debated and voted upon at any meeting may not be raised again until at least three, perhaps more, months have elapsed. The purpose of this standing order is to prevent constant repetition of debates and changing of decisions from one meeting to another. Something which would be destructive of the organisation's ability to progress. Suspension of the relevant standing order requires that it be moved, seconded and supported by at least a two thirds majority of those present and voting.

Fortified with a good knowledge of standing orders, and having thoroughly read all the papers, you set out confidently for your first meeting. You have a few points you would like to raise on agenda matters but may find that 'to speak or not to speak, is the problem.' Old timers on the committee may advise you that new members should be 'seen and not heard' until they have duly served their apprenticeship, or until 'you have got your legs under the table.' Perhaps reasonable advice but rather depressing to someone who wishes to use every opportunity to improve speaking ability. To comply with this advice could be dangerous to your development.

If you keep quiet during the first few meetings you will inevitably find it difficult to suddenly break out of your self-inflicted silence. So speak as soon as you have something worthwhile to contribute - but it must be worthwhile. For, until you speak, members will not know whether you are a fool or a philosopher. Your contribution should at least suggest you belong in the second category.

Listen to the comments of the longer serving and more experienced members before putting your own point of view. 'We have two ears and one mouth,' goes the old Greek proverb, 'so that we may listen the more and talk the less.' If you impetuously rush to take the lead in discussion you may take the wrong line, or show you do not fully understand the matter under discussion. To then be corrected by the more knowledgeable members will place you in the category of fool – and it will be difficult to later convince them otherwise.

Especially if, as many new members do, you have tried to make an impact by attacking the traditional views of the older hands.

Wait patiently until the more senior of your colleagues have spoken. You will then get an indication of what is the general line of thought and a few words of support will bring approval of your wisdom. Refrain from the usual sport of attacking the officers, for that might result in enmity that is difficult to overcome in the future. However misguided you believe they are, always remember they have probably given long service and have considerable collective wisdom. This should be respected by any intelligent newcomer. It is also valuable that your first speech should have a smooth passage. If it does, and perhaps even draws compliments, this will greatly help your confidence. But an angry rebuttal of your first effort will make you unsure about speaking again. To be a top class speaker implies not only good preparation and presentation skills, but also an understanding of and tolerance for your fellow human beings.

Any committee will comprise members who accept the responsibility of working together for the benefit of their organisation. Unfortunately there are others who conduct themselves as if their fellow members were opponents to be constantly challenged. If you want to excel on committee you must be able to understand and appreciate these traits in your fellow members, to know when it is necessary to oppose the windbag and when to support the more positive members. This is when the training of your mind (see Chapter 14) is essential to become a good, thoughtful and persuasive speaker.

Realise that it is entirely counter-productive to seek to 'demolish' someone during a debate, even if they are misguided. It is not a worthwhile objective. You and your unhappy victim are likely to be committee associates for some time. An immediate debating triumph may therefore be bought at the expense of future constructive relationships. There never is a time when a speech should include personal attacks or acrimony. Such an approach does not endear you to anyone. It will, on the contrary, dismay even those you have attracted as your supporters. A courteous speaking manner will gain general approval, lessen your opponent's chagrin if he loses the debate, and perhaps prevent him becoming an implacable enemy.

It is important you make as few enemies as possible if you wish to progress to being elected to office, for intellectual ability alone may not be sufficient. You very much need the respect and friendship of others. You should be aware, for example, when not to speak so as to avoid dominating discussions. For no one admires the 'know all', even if he does! As you gain respect and maturity you should, in fact, be trying to encourage the newer or more nervous members to speak and to help them do this. If you must oppose or compliment someone then do it as recommended by the old Russian statesman who said: 'I praise loudly and I blame softly.' If during the progress of debate you suddenly see that an earlier view you expressed is wrong, then say this and compliment the other speakers for clarifying the issue. They will feel flattered and friendly and you will have increased, not decreased, your reputation for integrity.

This is very important if you hope that some day your colleagues will entrust you with a senior position, such as committee chairman. They will do so with goodwill if they know they can rely on your impartiality and willingness to acknowledge fallibility. Your attitude to the existing chairman will also, if it is constructive, help convince them of this. A chairman has a difficult job, especially when controlling an important debate in which some members resort to acrimony. He should be supported if at all possible, because a chairman who feels secure in the position is good for the efficient conduct of the committee's business. He may make mistakes, as you might if occupying the chair. Treat him as you hope others would treat you. To try and expose the chairman to ridicule (a favourite pastime of some committee members) is to expose your own weakness. This will be noted by others, who will then show you no mercy if you ever make committee chairmanship.

Some of a committee's business is fairly formal: to receive and approve minutes, to deal with correspondence, to approve reports. Debates take place when a member proposes that a certain policy, or course of action, is adopted by moving a motion to this effect. If seconded by another member the discussion begins. Committee debates may not be as critical or tense as those within political parties or in front of a public audience, but it is still essential to prepare well and project your case skilfully. This guarantees that, with the limited time available, the most important points of your proposal will not be missed out. Having brief guide notes also safeguards against others misrepresenting your views. During the debate, for example, there may be someone who - perhaps because he has not listened carefully - will attack you because he has completely misunderstood your remarks. If you have written notes to hand these can be used to refute and clarify the matter when replying to the debate. And because of this right to reply you should also be taking note, during discussion of your motion, of any important opposition points so you can deal with them.

The right of reply does not give you the chance to make another speech in support of your proposal. The standing orders will usually specify that, in the right of reply, only points raised during debate may be commented upon and the proposer cannot introduce any new material. The technique in a right of reply speech is to deal with only those opposition points that might affect people's support for your proposal. Often during a debate it ranges so widely, and views are expressed which are irrelevant to the issue, that some committee members lose sight of what the motion is actually proposing. Of course the chairman should ensure this does not happen but all too frequently he does. The proposer in winding up the debate should therefore recap on the main terms of his motion, and not be drawn into replying to the irrelevancies.

There may be amendments to a motion which is before the meeting. The technique in speaking to these, and the speech preparation, is the same as for original proposals. All debates of this kind involve considerable expertise. The speaker must observe the courtesies of the platform debater, tempered by the knowledge of his long term position on the committee and the continuing relationship with his colleagues. Whatever divisions may arise over policies all members are supposed to be giving their time and thought for the common good in a democratically controlled organisation. Many top class speakers served their speaking apprenticeship through serving on committees. It is a good precedent for you to follow.

Meet The Media

If you are a speaker who needs a live audience to feed from, you may find it a lonely and difficult job if asked to do a radio or television broadcast. There is no immediate audience to give stimulus and atmosphere, and you will be uncomfortably aware that potential watchers and listeners could number millions. The usual, exuberant platform manner would jar on them for they will be receiving the broadcast in their homes. The style must be that of the friend calling in for a chat, the voice low-pitched and conversational. Because of the intimacy of sound or sight broadcasting the audience will be more aware of any mistakes or mannerisms which betray nerves. All this, coupled with the pace and urgency of broadcasting, adds up to additional tension for even the professional speaker.

Any speech, whether to the media or from the platform, should be crafted so that no words are wasted. This need to speak succinctly applies even more to radio and TV broadcasts. If given time before a broadcast it is wise to refine, in your mind, responses to the possible interview questions. Go over them until they are embedded in the memory and can then be produced effortlessly when you're in the studio. This kind of exercise also helps sharpen mental reaction for those occasions when there is little time for preparation. This frequently happens when some news item of importance surfaces and you are one of the 'experts' urgently requested to give a comment.

A common reaction to stress is temper or aggression. Not only will that be quickly perceived by the audience but an interviewer saddled with a recalcitrant, suspiciously hostile interviewee will cut short his disagreeable job. And you won't be invited again. So if you accept an invitation to speak on radio or TV you must attune yourself to the job in hand, keep your temper and prepare well. You must make every word count, so forget the usual opening courtesies of the public meeting. Get on with your message and drive it home as effectively as you can.

In a sound broadcast it is the quality of the message and the voice which are all important. The facial expressions and the mannerisms which would help emphasise your words on TV have to be conveyed entirely through the voice on radio. The listeners will judge whether you seem to have integrity, or are untrustworthy, by the way you speak. Get the right tone of voice, be capable of varying it to maintain interest, and don't appear too hesitant or suspicious in your replies to questions. Talk to the interviewer as if he were a trusted friend and that's how you will come over to others. Avoid vocal inflections that make you sound pompous, avuncular, sonorous or like a canting church minister. The dropped voice, or dying fall, at the end of a sentence is irritating to listeners and makes you sound insincere.

Listen to the professional broadcasters for examples to follow. Though their accents or pitch of voice may differ they have certain things in common: they usually speak a little quicker than in normal conversation, they don't hesitate between words, and they don't fill any gaps with 'er' or 'um.' Before the broadcast the sound technician will ask you to say a few words for him. This voice test enables him to adjust his equipment so the right vocal strength goes out during the broadcast. For the test you should use the pitch, strength and tone of voice with which you are most comfortable. If you do the test while slightly leaning on the table between you and the interviewer, don't then change position when the broadcast starts. For if you then lean forward your voice will be louder than in the test. If you lean back in your chair it will sound distant as if the interview is taking place at long range. Either way the sound technician will be given some anxious moments as he urgently adjusts his equipment. If you constantly shift in your seat his anxiety will last for the whole of the broadcast - and he will be hoping not to see you again in the studio.

One benefit of radio, opposed to TV, is that the listeners cannot see you. You can take off your jacket and tie if it makes you more comfortable. Sound studios don't have the hot, bright lights of a television set but they are effectively sealed against external noises and can be very warm. Your interviewer is also likely to be in shirt sleeves. If you don't get comfortable before you go on the air it will not be possible to do so after the broadcast starts, however hot and sticky you become.

You may be chatting casually with the interviewer just before going on the air but, when the red light comes on, your tone must immediately switch into the more authoritative style to deal with questions from him. If you conduct yourself like a professional he will be very happy; it makes his job a relatively easy one and it should be a good broadcast. Be ready to give him small but useful nuggets of information in reply to questions. He won't want to be like a prospector anxiously digging for gold in a mountain of useless ore.

Don't speak too long when replying to points. It's an interview, not a monologue, and the interviewer will want to come in frequently. It's his job to put the kind of questions that a listener might ask if he were in the studio. A long meandering answer from you may veer away from the area of the subject he's interested in, and it does not sound good if you are forcibly stopped speaking no matter how gently it is done. Certainly you should not use this technique as a deliberate ploy to evade questions which you find potentially embarrassing. The interviewer will not be fooled and is likely to become hostile, and your tactic will be irritating to listeners.

The same advice is relevant to a TV interview. Be well prepared, and short and to the point in your answers. On TV it is not only your voice but your dress and mannerisms which convey your image, good or bad, to the viewer. Dress, as you will have noticed from the TV screen, is fairly formal in most interviews. Reasonable but not flashy clothes for a woman, discreet suit and tie for a man. Avoid shiny materials that may appear very strange when transmitted by the cameras, or prove distracting to the viewer. There are certain things the studio can do to help your appearance before you go on show but a change of clothing is not one of them.

When you sit down in your seat on the set don't slump back. It does not appear professionally casual but gives the impression of lethargy, and sometimes truculence. Sit forward slightly as if ready for the business in hand. You will have noticed that some TV news readers lean forward, hands on their desk, to give the impression of alertness and urgency. But if you lean forward too much it might give you a hunched look, and this will be exaggerated if your suit or dress collar rises round the back of your neck. When you reply to questions do so in a calm, considered voice. You may, if necessary, pause slightly – very slightly - to look thoughtful as this can impress viewers. But the long pause, so effective on a public platform, is out.

Most interviewers are friendly and understand that you may be feeling nervous. It is in their interest, and that of the programme, to put you at ease and capable of making a good contribution. They will be delighted if you exceed their expectations and come up with interesting and newly minted pieces of information. You should perfect a few before getting to the studios. But you may meet the TV reporter or newsreader who, after speaking in neutral tones when introducing the item, suddenly turns to you and slips into his Robin Day impersonation. His face may twist into expressions of disbelief, sarcasm or hostility as he goes into his routine. You will have seen at least one in action on TV. "Do you really expect us to believe that, Mr. Commissioner," he sneers. "Can you actually look direct into the camera and tell viewers that you're satisfied with what your staff are doing?" It's a thoroughly unprofessional attitude, particularly for a reporter, because it casts serious doubt on his integrity and objectivity.

Papers are often accused of bias in the presentation of news stories, but think of the criticism there would be if reporters wrote them in the same subjective and combative style of some news broadcasters. If you have to face this kind of inquisition the right response is to continue calmly answering the questions - although the bull terrier approach of the reporter may include interrupting your remarks to put you off course. Persevere, and ultimately he will look like the amateur while you will appear the more professional.

Do not in any event consider the full-time TV journalist/ reporter as the ultimate professional. Some of them are bad models to emulate, and most oft-heard clichés are trotted out by them. These are not confined to the spoken word but extend to the visual shots taken by the camera crew. Many outside interviews open by showing us a walking figure. MPs are seen strolling across College Green, and business men on the streets outside their office, all self-consciously demonstrating they have effective use of their lower limbs before showing they can also speak. Yet this very worn camera cliché seems not to disturb the programme controllers, or suggest to them that if time is important it should be devoted to hearing what the interviewee has to say.

When invited to appear on TV don't think your spot is as important to the studio staff as it is to you. They will usually be very busy with their own concerns as they fine-tune the programme which is to go out. So after the excitement of getting to the studio you may be met rather perfunctorily and have to wait around for some time before a brief visit to the make-up room. Here they will powder any shiny spots on forehead, nose or cheeks which could reflect badly on camera, and discreetly hide the stubble marks of the men. TV cameras seem to accentuate this. No matter how smooth chinned you think you are, unless you have just shaved the cameras may make you look like a devotee of the 'designer stubble' fad.

When you finally arrive on the set try to look at ease, and have a slightly pleasant facial expression. But don't take it to extremes; a simpering, ingratiating smile does not look good. And remember the occasional example of people who are invited to give an eye witness account of some tragic accident. Either through nerves or pleasure at being on TV they appear to be grinning broadly while recounting details of the horrendous story.

When responding to questions speak directly to the person asking them. Resist turning aside to look at the camera, for this appears artificial and you seem to be ignoring the interviewer. Don't wave your arms about to emphasise a point. Study the interviewer, he will be sitting at ease with his hands in his lap or on the table in front of him. It may be that occasionally he will swivel in his chair to speak more directly to a guest, and indicate with his arm, but upper limb movements are not exaggerated.

Don't raise your voice: it shows temper, among other undesirable traits. Don't indulge in facial grimaces to emphasise your words. It is especially bad form to do this if someone else on the programme is speaking, and you are trying to convey a mute but hostile reaction to what they are saying. It does not come over well and is likely to antagonise the viewers, your fellow guest speaker, and the interviewer.

Don't preface your remarks with time wasting statements like "My personal view is ..." or "Well I think ..." That you are giving a personal view is accepted and the reason why you were invited to speak. And don't begin your replies with words like "Quite sincerely...." or "To be perfectly honest..." It achieves the opposite result; you will sound both insincere and dishonest.

Nor should you repeat the interviewer's question before replying to it. It is frequently a method of trying to gain a moment's additional time to think of a reply. Don't be influenced either by the growing trend for TV reporters to use it; it is still a very sloppy way of taking part in an interview. The newsreader, for example, introduces a report on some foreign danger zone then switches to the reporter on the spot.

"Would you say John that the position is very dangerous there at present?"

John pauses, looks gravely at the camera and replies: "Yes Charles, I would say that the position is very dangerous here at present because ..."

Back comes Charles: "So would you advise people at home not to travel there at present John?"

John looks into the camera. "Yes Charles, I would certainly advise people not to travel here at present because ..."

You might find yourself the 'man on the spot' getting interviewed on an outside broadcast. If you are you must speak directly at the hand held microphone. Keep turning your head and your voice will be heard in snatches. Resist the temptation to turn and point to some location relevant to the story - your voice will not then be heard at all. Neither should you use your hands to vigorously emphasise a point. The normal shot by the camera crew will be upwards from just below the chest. If your hands are in constant motion they will appear as unexplained little white blurs fluttering into the bottom of the picture. It is irritating and will distract the viewer's attention from what you are saying.

In an outside broadcast it is even more essential that you respond to questions with short but intelligent bursts of information. External conditions are not usually good for long interviews and your information is, in any event, likely to be a 'sound-bite' supporting the main news story.

Don't be surprised - though you may be upset - if having taken considerable trouble to get to the place of interview your contribution is drastically shortened when put out by the studio. Some of the early questioning is not intended to be broadcast but to get you into the right frame of mind and allow the sound technician to assess the correct level for recording your voice. Your interview might not even appear at all. One reason for this is that you were only a back-up choice for the news item. First choice was perhaps the more impressively titled Sir John Smith but, until late in the day, they were unable to contact him for an interview. Sir John is finally found and duly obliges. The TV studio has no remorse about throwing away your effort.

There are also times when pressure of late important news items means that all the others have to be shortened. If your piece is not critical then it, and perhaps the whole report, may end up in the studio dustbin. One way to avoid being too easily jettisoned is to ensure that you stick to all the guidelines for being a good interviewee. And then, even if you still end up having an aborted session, the producer may well remember your professional style and invite you back again.

Newspapers also form an important medium for mass contact between message and recipient. The reader has also more time to digest it, perhaps even keep the item filed if it is considered very important. A press interview has not the same terrors as TV or sound broadcast. It is more leisurely and, however rambling your response, it is the reporter's job to make it comprehensible before it is printed in the paper. This does not mean you should be less careful about preparation of your message. Don't give a press reporter a difficult time trying to make sense of your almost incoherent remarks. And do not deny those which, in print, you subsequently find embarrassing. You will be struck off his list of 'experts' to contact when next he wants an informed and apt quote on a specialist subject.

Up In The Gallery

'They are not particular in their dress; they even come into the House in their greatcoats, and with boots and spurs. It is not at all uncommon to see a member lying stretched out on one of the benches, while others are debating. Some crack nuts, others eat oranges or whatever else is in season. If it happens that a member rises who is but a bad speaker; or if what he says is generally deemed not sufficiently interesting, so much noise is made, and such bursts of laughter are raised, that the member who is speaking can scarcely distinguish his own words. The Speaker in his chair, like a tutor in a school, again and again endeavours to restore order, which he does by calling out 'to order, to order'; apparently often without much attention being paid to it.'

Not a comment on today's House of Commons! The rather jaundiced visitor to the gallery in 1782 was Carl Philipp Moritz, a German, who made a special point of going to see the 'Mother of Parliaments' in what was clearly less than impressive session. His comment is a rebuttal to the critics who lament the present standards of dress and conduct in today's House compared with the imagined decorum and dignity of the past.

A visitor to the Commons gallery today may still be unimpressed by the standard of speeches made by some members of what is considered the greatest debating chamber in the country – if not the world. But it is the goal of aspiring politicians, who may visit the gallery to see what, they hope, is an insight into their prospective future. Yet, unless it is a 'big day' the chamber will look deserted. The few members taking part in debate are perhaps lacklustre, addressing a government front bench on which sit a couple of lethargic junior ministers. The prospective MP, perhaps already a very competent platform speaker, is in no doubt that he could perform as well and perhaps better.

Attendance during a major debate will tend to convince him otherwise. The major speakers on both sides will be present, and the most important government ministers; the intellectual content of the speeches and the quality of debate well worthy of the best traditions of Parliament. Certainly not an arena into which a fledgling MP would enter with confidence. The occasional interjection of the aggressive loudmouth is an isolated example rather than the norm it may have been in the past. From these debates will frequently come a pungent comment or *bon mot* which echoes down the years. The prohibitions on using unparliamentary language has spawned quite a number as some MPs used their quick intellect, and ability to think on their feet, to evade the charge and avoid the wrath of the Speaker.

One of the best known examples is by Winston Churchill who, unable to call an opponent a liar, said instead that he was "guilty of a terminological inexactitude." Others are less adroit but just as effective. It may be said of a minister that: "He has just announced policies in which he has no real belief and, although he has declared his fervour for them, will not implement them if returned to power after the impending election." That is permissible. But to declare bluntly (though to the same effect) that he is a liar and a hypocrite, is not.

Because the House's traditions have been established over centuries it may take some time for a new member to absorb them, and also to understand the complex Parliamentary standing orders which govern debates. While not a rigid straight-jacket they do tend to curb the emotional, free ranging and informal speeches common to the public platform. New MPs can therefore find the House a very trying experience as they seek to establish their particular niche in it. That 'niche' is likely to be a sharp contrast to their election campaign, where they were given great prominence with all the publicity focused on them. Then, almost straight from the glamour and fervour of the polling night result, they arrive at Westminster to find they are nonentities.

They may have been outstanding public speakers but learn, right from their maiden speech to the House, that they must adapt to a mould more appropriate to Hansard, the official report. On the platform the unfinished sentence - deliberately left hanging as a question mark - the long pause or the rhetorical flourish may be appreciated by an attendant audience. The same speaking techniques result in something resembling gibberish when reported in Hansard. The new MP soon learns that his speeches have to be well prepared with the thoughts flowing smoothly, and his sentences must be rounded with no 'dying falls' at the end of them – or the Hansard note-takers will not pick them up. For similar reasons the MP with a strong regional accent will have to make it less pronounced.

This is why many early speeches in the House tend to be rather measured and without pretence to emotional oratory. It is also the reason why the first task of many MPs who have just spoken is to go up to the Hansard room to read the speech in typescript. The reporters will permit him or her to amend the grammar of the sentences but not the political views expressed, or the essence of the speech. Opportunity to amend style at reporting stage is why speeches sometimes read better in Hansard than they sounded when delivered in the House.

The challenge for the new back-bench speaker is to overcome these inhibitions and attune delivery to the parliamentary style without becoming tedious. Lack of speaking opportunity may delay progress towards this objective. It was once remarked that the best parliamentary speeches have never been delivered. This is because every member intending to speak will have thoroughly prepared his notes some time before the debate in which he is interested. This is, after all, the most eminent forum in which he participates and he wants to excel. Though MPs are not supposed to read from a script they may carry fairly detailed notes to keep them on course. The Member, already tense thinking of the coming ordeal, may then have to sit on the bench for some hours, listening to others and continually jumping up in the hope of 'catching the Speaker's eye'. If unsuccessful, and there are many disappointed hopefuls during a major debate, it means wasted preparation of there intended speech.

There might, however, be the opportunity of some slight recompense. Once the MP is fairly certain he will not be called he can try to get over a major point from his prepared notes by asking the minister, or member, who is speaking to 'give way.' He does this by rising to his feet, at the appropriate point for his intervention, and requesting them to give way. If willing to accept the interjection they sit down and invite him to put his point. It is one way to overcome total frustration and, if successful, at least guarantees his name will appear in Hansard. Perhaps in the daily papers if it is considered newsworthy.

The member or minister on their feet will think twice before giving way. They may know the MP making the request is an expert on the subject being debated, therefore capable of putting a point which will be difficult, or impossible, to answer off the cuff. They will not give him the opportunity to demonstrate his undoubted expertise at their expense, so might blandly respond that "My time is limited and I cannot therefore give way," or plead consideration for others. "I understand that many other Hon. Members wish to speak in this debate so I cannot give way as it will only prolong my speech, and reduce their opportunity of catching the Speaker's eye."

The consequent frustration for the back-bencher is increased by knowing that long serving MPs and ex-ministers will be given priority by the Speaker. Yet this is understandable for the Speaker wants the most expert contributions during debate on an important subject, and recognises that a great deal of knowledge and expertise exists among the ranks of former ministers and mature members. One way for the tyro to improve his or her chance to speak is by dropping a short note to the Speaker explaining that they have a specialist, or very considerable constituency, interest in the matter. That may not help if there already is a long list of hopefuls.

Ministers have a much easier passage. They know when they are billed to speak in a debate, and have all their department's resources at hand to help prepare their script. They also benefit from the air of authority given them because they are speaking on behalf of the government. The tradition that speeches are not read does not extend to ministers, and would be foolish if it did. Ministers make important announcements on behalf of government and any verbal slip, or impromptu remark capable of being misunderstood, can have serious consequences. Ministers have sometimes had to resign in such circumstances. So each one has his portfolio with him, lays it on the despatch box, and usually reads carefully from it.

The winding up ministerial speech, at the end of the day's

debate, requires greater expertise than the opening address from the front bench. The minister given the task is expected to sit through almost the whole of the debate, apart from a short break for refreshment, in order to hear the points made by the various speakers. It is his duty to reply to the most important of them, weaving them into his basic closing brief, which will have been prepared earlier. TV audiences are sometimes impressed at the learned manner in which he can deal with even the more erudite points that have been raised. But he has an invaluable aid that is not so noticeable to the onlooker in the gallery. To the right hand of the Speaker there is a box, rather like a church pew, in which sit departmental civil servants throughout the whole of the debate. If the minister wants factual material on any argument raised by a member he asks his parliamentary private secretary (PPS), who sits just behind him, to get it from these civil servants. The PPS walks along the bench to the box and gives them the note from the minister. Within a short time they will usually have compiled a reply. The minister may have this help with factual information, but the ability to fit them seamlessly into his winding up speech is entirely his.

    Opposition spokesmen are not so favoured. Though they have the assistance of research workers from their party offices, who sit at the other end of the House, the quality of information is not so good nor authoritative. That is because the research staff have not the same access to information, and there are usually only a few of them - with other work to do for their parties - compared with the top class civil service ranks from which ministers can seek advice.

    This is very evident during preparation for oral question sessions in the House – the most testing time for ministers. The questions will have been submitted earlier and then printed on the order paper for the day. In the department concerned the civil servants prepare the factual basis for the response to them. Before going to the House for the question session the minister studies these with the civil servants and rehearses the replies he will give. These are typed and placed in the folder that he carries with him. The testing time is not therefore the initial replies to questions. It is the supplementary follow up – allowed each MP who raises an oral question - and about which the minister may have no prior information. MPs, especially from the opposition, will almost always be hoping to confound him, thereby making their reputation at his expense.

The minister, at least as anxious about his own status, will wish to prevent this. During the earlier session with his civil servants they will attempt to foresee the possible supplementaries which might be based on the original oral question. If all else fails the minister's parliamentary private secretary will be sent on a 'fishing mission' to see if he can wheedle it out of the MP. This can be as successful as asking an enemy country to reveal details of its secret weapon!

House of Commons members represent a very wide selection of the general public; the educated and the uneducated; the rich and the poor; the religious and the irreligious; the intellectual and the very average mind. This is its strength, not its weakness. Parliamentary legislation is passed by MPs only when the interest of the groups they represent have been thoroughly considered, which means they will then become generally acceptable to the electorate. This implies that MPs are themselves of differing achievements and abilities. Yet not all the most outstanding orators or intellects make it to the front bench. Why? Some may be judged to be rather 'unreliable', too intellectually erratic or individualistic to be good members of the ministerial team. Or they may parade their talents a little too obviously. The point was succinctly put by another Churchill - Charles Churchill - over 200 hundred years ago:

> 'The danger chiefly lies in acting well;
> No crime's so great as daring to excel.'

Chapter 8 of this book highlighted the skills required to win debates, stressing the need for a courteous attitude to your opponent and that you should not respond to any insult or personal attack. Why then in the most important debating forum are these qualities noticeably lacking? The answer is that MPs are not debating one to one in front of an audience from which they seek support. The lobby votes at the end of their debates are predetermined, and the possibility of converting one of the opposition is remote almost to the point of impossibility. The primary objective of minister or MP is to gain approval from their own side. The back-bencher hopes to catch the attention of the Prime Minister or Chief Whip as potential ministerial candidate. Those who are already ministers hope to earn promotion. That is not to say that a courteous minister or MP lacks the appreciation of other members, but they must also be capable of the combat style of debate if they are to win prestige and advancement.

The House of Lords is a more contemplative chamber. It has some of the finest intellects in the country, and many ex-ministers with considerable government experience. There are also no constituency pressures on members, no need to fight a general election. Many of those who sit in the House are totally independent of any party. Ministerial office opportunities, or those for opposition spokesmen, are limited and not so fiercely sought in any event. The cut and thrust, and the insults, of an elected chamber are therefore normally absent from the Lords. So it is there one can hear debates which are usually rancour free, and genuinely seek to persuade. It is also there that one more frequently hears the best oratory; a combination of vocal ability and a keen intellect working in tandem.

'Democracy' is defined as a state in which there is government of the people by the people through the ballot box. But the essence of a democracy is not simply that every adult has a vote at elections; people must also be able to express their views freely. The right to these freedom's is important for any civilised country, and many people have died to preserve those we have in the United Kingdom. It is therefore sad that the great majority allow others to think and speak for them. Only relatively few people are prepared to study or enter into politics and to equip themselves to take part in the great debate. The result is that, while our society may be classed as a democracy, it cannot be said to be a very informed one. Those who do think of the political issues, and school themselves to speak about them, contribute greatly to the preservation of effective democracy.

Yet, with all its faults, democracy is the only acceptable form of social and political organisation for a nation. Not because it is 'efficient' in the usual commercial or business sense, but on the principle that stable and enlightened societies can only be built on the right of each person to express his or her views.

The building of our roads and industrial and commercial developments could proceed much faster, and at more economical cost, if we did not have planning laws which enable people to object to the point of seriously delaying or stopping such projects. This public right of expression is certainly in sharp contrast to the situation that existed in the fascist states of Germany and Italy before the last war. There were people throughout Europe who admired Hitler and Mussolini because they so speedily constructed the first extensive motorway systems, and re-generated the structural and industrial organisation of their countries. But the price paid in the loss of personal and intellectual freedom was too high, and the example of Germany and Italy simply proved once again that unelected regimes are always unstable and will ultimately collapse - as they have also done in the eastern block countries in recent years.

Winston Churchill most effectively put the case for democracy in a speech he made in 1947: "Many forms of government have been tried," he said, "and will be tried in this world of sin and woe. No one pretends that democracy is perfect or all-wise. Indeed it has been said that democracy is the worst form of government except all those other forms that have been tried from time to time."

Keeping Them Awake

The perfect recipe for sleep? An abundance of good food, liberal supplies of alcohol - and a droning after dinner speaker. If the ingredients could be distilled and bottled, a fortune could be made from sales to despairing insomniacs! But too often the combination results in bad tempered heckling from those made argumentative by alcohol, while the rest of the guests talk among themselves in preference to listening to a boring speech in which few others are interested.

The American comedian Alben Barkley once said that "The best audience is one that is intelligent, well educated - and a little drunk." It is doubtful whether that is really typical of American experience. In the UK that type of audience is certainly difficult even for the most accomplished speaker. At worst there are likely to be dinner tables where men, spurred by too much wine, try to impress their female companions by talking loudly and telling jokes while the speaker is on his feet. The ladies, equally 'merry,' laugh loudly at their supposed witticisms. The MC may glare, bang his gavel, appeal for quiet – to be met only by the giggles of the offenders who may or may not respond by a few moments silence. No MC or chairman can make a reasoning appeal to minds made unreasoning by drink.

Excessive alcohol and an attentive audience are incompatible. Either those who indulge quietly nod off to sleep or continue to have a little fun at the poor speaker's expense. Nor is there any way to stop it, short of throwing the troublemakers out of the room. This rarely happens because it would only create an even greater disturbance. Usually the only effective counter measure is to ensure the offenders are not sold tickets for future events. One way to try and avoid this trouble is for the speaker to aim at immediately attracting and retaining the interest of the audience; to keep them awake and interested. It is not easy, especially if the speech cannot simply be a recitation of jokes but has more serious content such as proposing a toast or vote of thanks.

The comedian or entertainer asked to speak at stag nights or specialist dinners is usually more fortunate in not having to be concerned about interesting ways to present the more formal material. These professionals - comedians, star sportsmen, athletes or other well known personalities - are also able to perfect their delivery because of the number of times they give the same speech. Just like the old days, when an entertainer could live on the same act for a continual circuit of the music halls (then TV came in and ate up his material in one broadcast).

The amateur has no opportunity to fine-tune his speech through repetition. His first may well be his last for some time. And because it is easier to simply tell a few jokes he may be tempted to do this and only add a few obligatory serious remarks at the end. Sometimes these may be forgotten in the excitement and pleasure he gets from making the audience laugh, so he sits down without carrying out this most important duty. The Master of Ceremonies then leans over to whisper in his ear, and he has to rise again to apologise and give the formal toast. It is a sorry end to the speech and there will be criticism, even from those who laughed at the jokes, that the speaker forgot to say anything about the association or the special people to be thanked.

The well constructed speech, including humour but also carrying out the essential courtesies, may be more difficult to prepare and deliver but will certainly be appreciated and remembered if it is done well. The after dinner speech is a curious convention which many speakers find off-putting. Even MPs have been heard to confess they would rather face a Parliamentary select committee than make one. But no prestigious occasion is complete unless it has a toast list of important guests. Each will have been impressed by the organisers that the greatest desire of all attending is to hear them speak ... but, please, for as short a time as possible. Only at special dinners for businessmen, or organisations like literary and debating societies, is the guest speaker expected to deliver an expert address of twenty minutes or so after the meal.

The amateur usually faces the toughest task: a mixed audience at what is his first big occasion, perhaps the annual dinner dance of his local association. He knows the women will be uninterested in a long speech about the state of the economy as it affects the Worthy

Association of Tinsmiths – of which he has the honour of presenting a toast as the newly elected president of the branch. The speeches will be regarded by most guests as a tedious interval between the meal and the dance. But the Tinsmith's members will expect him to say at least a few words relative to the toast he has to propose. Getting the balance right is difficult for the experienced; it is a sore trial for the amateur. As previous chapters have emphasised, preparation is all important. With only a few minutes to speak every word must count. The speech must be like a fast moving train that goes straight along the tracks to its destination *without any detours or getting side-tracked from the script in front of the speaker.*

Some find this very difficult, and frequently it is the amateur who offends by failure to stick to his notes. As he is speaking he suddenly happens to think of some exciting event that has just happened in the Tinsmith's world and breaks into his prepared speech to let his totally disinterested guests know about it. If they are very unfortunate he will perhaps have a few more 'de-railments' before the long awaited conclusion. So the first advice is to stick to the speech outlined in your notes and keep at it until you reach its destination.

These notes should be prepared after the speaker has confirmed for how long he is to speak; the exact words of the toast to be made; the type of audience; the numbers of people who will be present; if there will be a microphone and the name/s of the people to be coupled with the toast. Write or print them legibly, and if there are any unusual ones make sure you have the correct pronunciation. This is particularly relevant when there may be important foreign guests present because of the number of European Community organisations in the commercial and industrial sectors.

There are also the occasions when as a distinguished guest, invited to propose a toast to an organisation, you have no intimate knowledge of its history. The secretary should be able to let you have the appropriate details. The main points should be included in your speech but don't be tempted to go into too much detail; the audience has no wish to be bored with your newly acquired historical knowledge. If you can discover some little known point about the association's history this is usually appreciated, and will show you have taken the trouble to research the facts. Your background information will also enable you to talk about the association in a confident manner.

Some outside speakers invited to propose a toast are obviously under-prepared and, because of this, afraid of making an unqualified statement. They preface every remark with 'I think' or 'I believe.' Example: "I believe 1983 was your 50th anniversary year." Or: "I think it was in 1908 that your association was first formed." This doubt on the speaker's part is not complimentary to his audience. Get your facts right, state them boldly, and it will impress your listeners.

Humour in a speech is always appreciated and even the non-Tinsmith's members will sit up and listen if it is entertaining. In a mixed company it will help keep the ladies attentive. But the humour must be carefully chosen. Don't recycle old jokes which many of them may already know. Blue jokes are in bad taste and should be left out because, irrespective of the laughter they may raise, there will be many who resent them. It is also a mistake to make self-deprecatory jokes unless the company knows you well. Too often the joke is really self-complimentary and eased in under the guise of the speaker poking fun at himself. Or it may be that the speaker is trying to ingratiate himself with the audience. Either way his listeners can usually see through this ploy.

It is much more effective if, instead of telling straight jokes, you try to adapt them to make a topical comment about the association or its officers. Comedians give their jokes topicality and punch by doing this. Books like *The Toastmaster's Treasure Chest*, by Herbert V Prochnow, are very useful as a source of material for this type of humorous approach. With a little thought they can help put over the more formal, important information about the association which invited you to speak. For example: one epigram it contains reads that 'If you look like your passport photo, you aren't well enough to travel!'

This could be the basis for a humorous speech: "I am pleased to congratulate the association on its emergence as a power within the new European Federation of Tinsmiths, and also to specially mention John Martin who has been appointed as your delegate to its central committee. When he went to Brussels for its first meeting the Belgian immigration officer carefully studied his passport, taken when John was rather more youthful, and said: "This doesn't look very much like you."

"John, ever ready with a British Bon motte, replied: 'Well you know what they say, if you look like your passport photo you're not fit enough to travel."

"The immigration officer looked rather sourly at him, slid the passport back and grunted: 'Is that so? Then you should have stayed at home.'"

With this little story you have introduced a humorous note, showed that you knew of the association's new European role, and the part being played by one of its officers. You can also unfailingly raise a laugh by changing the format of a well-known cliché to give it a surprise ending. For example: at a dinner dance it is traditional to praise the ladies for the support they give to their businessmen husbands ("behind every successful man stands a good and supportive woman").

Traditional yes, also a little trite. The compliment can be conveyed in a humorous way without detracting from its sincerity. "As everyone knows," you begin, "behind every successful man stands ..." The audience smiles in anticipation of the usual ending. But you pause and add: "a woman who never has anything to wear!" Or "Behind every successful businessman stands ... a very surprised mother-in-law!" The surprise ending usually jolts the audience into laughter and applause, especially from the women!

You have almost reached the end of your speech and, just before the formal toast, have been asked to mention a few special guests. These, from your earlier preparations will be written on the notes in front of you. Do not mention them in falling order of importance then, before the final name, preface it by the traditional: "And last, but not least...."

This is a silly and needless phrase which means exactly the opposite. The last name mentioned by most speakers is usually of the least important person in the line up. The audience, and the person named, will know you are simply being condescending. If you have to include anyone in a toast then just do it. If you want to make your speech a little out of the ordinary you could leave the most important person to the last. First give a few complimentary words to the various people you have been asked to mention, then add: "I now turn to George Smith. He is the secretary of the branch and the committee which organised this wonderful banquet and ball. He has been the chief motivator of the local Tinsmith's association and has a wise and guiding hand in all its affairs. We therefore owe a particular debt of gratitude to him. I am sure you will agree that he and all the others I have mentioned have done a splendid job of work."

In this little speech nobody has been downgraded and everyone knows the last person mentioned is clearly the most important. And among the rest there has been no discernible pecking order. Everyone's honour will have been satisfied.

A valuable tip about doing the actual toast to an organisation; first find out how many members of the organisation are at the event. If you give it as traditional: "I now ask every member of the Worthy Association of Tinsmiths to rise with me and drink a toast to the organisation and to our guests," you may find a few lone, embarrassed figures rising here and there. A visible sign of the weakness of the organisation, and that most people present are guests or guests of a guest. The solution, which will always meet with approval from the officials, is to say something like: "I now ask every member of the Worthy Association of Tinsmiths and their honoured guests to rise with me and drink a toast ..."

The usual after dinner speech is allowed only a few minutes. Even the amateur may feel he can manage without notes for such a short effort. But it is still advisable to have notes or a script to keep you determinedly on course. Have them written or printed so you can read them easily. The letters should be large enough to be read if they are to be left on the table – not many speakers like the audience to see them closely reading from a script in their hand. Put them in front of the microphone stand. You can then casually glance at them as you speak into it. If you lay the notes immediately in front of you on the table it means you have to break off your speech, bend your head to look down and then back up again to the mike. This certainly draws attention to them.

Excessive notes will warn an audience that a long, boring speech is on the way. Particularly if the speaker first gets up, totally unprepared for the MC's call, and starts fumbling in all his pockets for the elusive and voluminous notes. He then has to arrange them in order, meanwhile apologising to all and sundry, before droning away monotonously and at a snail's pace. The apprehension of the audience resigned to a long boring speech is well known - and traded upon by the speaker who makes a joke of it in the hope of raising an easy laugh. "I was asked to keep things going for an hour or so," he will grin, holding up a large bundle of notes (some have been known to pretend they have so many notes they've been written on a toilet roll), "but I'll do you a favour and cut it short." At this point the 'notes' are flamboyantly thrown aside to the applause of the audience. Yes; it's all been done before – many times - and is not worth repeating.

Never apologise for the time you are taking: "I am not going to be too long." Or: "I am nearing my conclusion now and won't be much longer." It's a sign of weakness: just get on with what you have to say. Using some of your valuable time to explain you will not be taking too much of it is self-defeating, and shortens the time you have for your actual speech. One exception to this rule is the very humorous introduction by American General W.C. Westmoreland to a mixed audience. "I am sorry my wife is unwell and cannot be here tonight. So may you be. Usually she sits in the audience looking sweetly at me then, after a little, she may throw me a kiss. People think we must be very affectionate. Actually it's a private code: K-I-S-S – keep it short stupid!"

Nor should you begin by apologising for your lack of experience. It is often a rather fruitless attempt to ingratiate yourself with the audience. But you won't enlist their sympathy by pleading that you are 'not used to this sort of thing,' or 'I must apologise for the fact that I am not a very good speaker.' Your audience will only feel sympathy for themselves at having to listen to your stumbling efforts. As humorist Kim Hubbard once said: "Why don't the feller who says 'I'm not a speechmaker' let it go at that instead of givin' a demonstration?"

You will neither have to apologise for over-running your time, or for being amateurish, if you carefully prepare your notes and constantly rehearse them for time and vocal delivery. This should be at the speed you will use when addressing the audience. Keep refining them until they fit the length of time you have been given to speak. The rehearsal will also fix them in your mind and give you the best intonation for delivery. Prune the most inessential points if it looks as if you might over-run. This will probably make the speech even more concise and pithy. If you have to make a special mention of any people, or are including humorous remarks, remember to allow a few moments for the hopefully expected applause or the laughter this will bring.

But it may well be your first speech and you are too nervous to attempt jokes, humour, or even to keep going for more than a few minutes. This daunting fate usually awaits the newly elected chairman of an organisation when he presides over its annual dinner dance. His previous speaking efforts will have been at committee or branch attended by only a few of the faithful. Now he is confronted by a mixed audience of a hundred or more. Adequate preparation will help you to get up and do the job as well and as sincerely as possible.

And most of your audience will, because they know you, understand the tension and effort the speech has cost you. If you can only remain on your feet for a short time make that time effective. Your notes should be conveniently laid out in front of you so that you can turn over a page without having to fumble with them. Take a deep breath, be ready for the announcement by the MC, then get up and at them. – like a thoroughbred out of the starting gate.

There will be sympathy for you as a new boy without the need to plead for it by explaining "you are not used to this sort of thing." And your final consolation? It has never been known for an audience to complain because an after dinner speech was too short!

Gifts From The Greeks

The pen is mightier than the word. No, that is not a misprint! Spoken language is certainly very important, and the first humans who struggled to form a systematic and recognisable verbal means of communication rendered a great service to mankind. But the invention of a method of setting this down in a permanent form - attributed to the Sumerian's about 4000 BC - was of much greater importance for the development of civilisation. Literature, science, technology and the arts would have remained in a very primitive state if passed down the ages only by word of mouth.

It is written communication, and particularly since invention of the printing press, that has enabled each generation to build upon the achievements of the past. It is our most valuable heritage, and students of the arts, sciences or literature go automatically to the books which are a distillation of all previous knowledge on these subjects. But few students of public speaking, even the most experienced platform performers, trouble to read the thoughts and orations of the greatest statesmen over the past 2500 years.

This may be because of an assumption by some that our present standards of oratory are, like the developments in science, art and technology, advanced far beyond those of the past. This is certainly not true. In ancient Greece the art of speaking was brought to a peak, and vigorously encouraged by all who loved learning. To be an esteemed orator was to have an established place in public life and in the opinion of the general public. Some of the Greek orations still stand as brilliant examples of what can be achieved through a combination of the intellect and the spoken word.

Among the best speakers in Parliament or public life are the relatively few who have had a classical education, or have individually turned to the orations of the Greeks for inspiration. Certainly the speaker who wishes to excel will find no greater learning examples of the most simple, but supremely effective, ways to express one's thoughts than those speeches which come down to us from over two thousand years ago. A few brief extracts from the most famous Greek orations, and the modern's who learned from them, are given below.

The link between them is that they were all delivered at a particular time in history. The were made when, perhaps, the state was under threat; or the speakers were expressing a philosophy which was very advanced for that age and could - and occasionally did - cost them their lives. Among the more recent statesmen in British history, who carried on the classical style of oratory, are Edmund Burke, Disraeli and Churchill. To show how they made use of the 'gifts from the Greeks' a few examples from their most noted orations are given.

Their speeches also have force because of the dramatic times in which each of these men lived. Burke was acknowledged to be perhaps the finest speaker since the days of the most famous Greek orator, Demosthenes, (although Burke's delivery was sometimes less perfect than his content). Churchill followed the classical mould, his intellect and vocal ability in perfect tune. His orations could instruct, inspire - and tingle the blood.

Serious students of the spoken word do themselves a disservice if they ignore the masters of the past. Study each of the examples below. Note how dramatic effect is achieved by an apparently simple – but extremely skilful - turn of speech to excite the intellect.

Pericles

Born in 490 BC Pericles was the outstanding statesman of his day and held the post of Athenian general-in-command for many years. He innovated improvements in public works and civil policies, and showed great concern for the advancements of the arts. He was a brilliant example of the soldier/ philosopher, whose intellect roamed freely over the whole field of human endeavour. One of his finest speeches was given as the funeral oration in praise of his countrymen who were killed in an important battle. For what kind of country, he pondered, and for what ideals had they died? In trying to provide the answer Pericles stated a theory of society, and the place of man within it, which still serves as a model for today. He said:

"The constitution by which we live does not emulate the enactment's of our neighbours. It is an example to others rather than an imitation of them. It is called democracy because power does not rest with the few, but with the many, and in law, as it touches individuals, all are equal, while in regard to the public estimation in which each man is held in any field, his advancement depends not on mere rotation, but rather on his true worth; nor does poverty dim his reputation or prevent him from assisting the state, if he has the capacity. Liberty marks both our public politics and the feelings which touch our daily lives together ... We are seekers of beauty, but avoid extravagance; of learning, but without unmanliness. For us wealth is an aim for its value in use and not as an empty boast, and the disgrace of poverty rests not in the admission of it, but more in the failure to avoid it in practice. It lies with all to superintend home life and state affairs alike, while despite our varied concerns we keep an adequate acquaintance with politics. We alone regard the man who takes no part in it, not as unobtrusive, but as useless, and we all at least give much thought to an action, if we do not rightly originate it, supposing not that it is debate which is the undoing of action, but rather the lack of debate to warn us before it."

Socrates

Socrates was born in Athens in 469 BC at a time when that city was emerging as a great nation state under the leadership of Pericles. The ascendancy of the Athenians brought a new vigour to every form of public and private life, in which great importance was laid upon the ability to speak well. Socrates is justifiably claimed to be among those who shaped the intellectual development of the West. Yet he committed nothing to paper. It is Plato, his disciple and admirer, who mainly reported the speeches and thought of Socrates so that we are able to read them today.

Plato also made it clear that Socrates had an interrogative form of discussion which antagonised many of his fellow citizens, and ultimately brought him to trial for his life at the age of seventy. Facing a jury of 501 fellow Athenians, Socrates himself acknowledged that he was "fairly certain that this plain speaking of mine is the cause of my unpopularity." This did not prevent him from continuing the same course at his trial.

When finally sentenced to death, and even under the great stress of that moment, he did not waver from the intellectual honesty that distinguished his life. His valuable speech at that time, emphasising the high moral conduct which he thought should motivate mankind, is perhaps encapsulated as preferring 'death rather than dishonour'. He told those who had condemned him to death that:

"You would have liked to hear me weep and wail, doing and saying all sorts of things which I regard as unworthy of myself, but which you are used to hearing from other people. But I did not think then that I ought to stoop to servility because I was in danger, and I do not regret the way in which I pleaded my case; I would much rather die as a result of this defence than live as a result of the other sort. In a court of law, just as in warfare, neither I nor any other ought to use his wits to escape death by any means. In battle it is often obvious that you could escape being killed by giving up your arms and throwing yourself upon the mercy of your pursuers; and in every kind of danger there are plenty of devices for avoiding death if you are unscrupulous enough to stick at nothing. But I suggest gentlemen, that the difficulty is not so much to escape death; the real difficulty is to escape from doing wrong, which is far more fleet of foot. In this present instance I, the slow old man, have been overtaken by the slower of the two, but my accusers have been overtaken by the faster: by iniquity. When I leave this court I shall go away condemned by you to death, but they will go away convicted by Truth herself of depravity and wickedness."

Demosthenes

Born 85 years after Socrates, Demosthenes suffered the same fate of death by having to drink poison. He is regarded as the most outstanding Greek orator, and some claim he is the greatest of all time. He constantly urged the Athenians to join with other Greek states to oppose the growing imperial ambitions of Phillip of Macedon, father of Alexander the Great. He paid for this with his life. The following extract is from a speech he made, when opposing Phillip's imperial ambitions, in which he gave his view on democracy as opposed to oligarchy.

"Our country has been engaged in numerous wars, against democracies as well as oligarchies. You know this well enough. But the motive of each of these encounters is perhaps a thing on which no one reflects. What is the motive? Against popular governments it has either been a matter of private grievances which could not be solved by public negotiation, or of partition of land, of boundaries, of community feeling or of leadership. Against oligarchies none of these considerations has applied; it has been an ideological matter or a question of liberty. Indeed, I would not hesitate to maintain that I think it better that all the Greeks should be our enemies under democracy than our friends under oligarchy. In dealing with free states, in my view, there is no difficulty about regaining peace, while with oligarchy even friendship is precarious. There can be no good feeling between oligarchy and democracy, between the desire for power and the aim at a life of equality ... the subversion of a political way of life and its change into oligarchy should be regarded, I urge, as fatal to all aspirations to freedom."

Edmund Burke

Burke is regarded as an orator in the traditions of the ancient Greeks. Born in 1729 he made an immediate impact on his Parliamentary colleagues with his first speech in the House of Commons in 1766. To the problems of his day he applied a mind which unfailing weighed the major moral principles involved, and his speeches contain lessons for us wherever they touch upon matters of contemporary concern. The following extract is from one he made in 1770 on the relationships between governments and the governed.

"I am not one of those who think that the people are never in the wrong. They have been so, frequently and outrageously, both in other countries and in this. But I do say, that in all disputes between them and their rulers, the presumption is at least upon a par in favour of the people. Experience may perhaps justify me in going further. When popular discontent's have been very prevalent, it may well be affirmed and supported, that there has been generally something found amiss in the constitution, or in the conduct of government. The people have no interest in disorder. When they do wrong, it is their error, and not their crime. But with the governing part of the state, it is far otherwise. They may certainly act ill by design, as well as by mistake ... If this presumption in favour of the subjects against the trustees of power be not the more probable, I am sure it is the more comfortable speculation; because it is more easy to change an administration than to reform a people."

Disraeli

Disraeli, born in 1804, was to become one of the most noted leaders of the Parliamentary Conservative Party and an acclaimed public speaker. Like the other orators quoted above, he examined the basic principles behind the issues of the day, rather than make mundane political speeches which skirted round contemporary problems. His speech in 1872, on 'The Principles of the Conservative Party' is a cogent example. He began by extolling the excellence of the British constitution and continued his argument that:

"Since the settlement of that constitution, now nearly two centuries ago, England has never experienced a revolution, though there is no country in which there has been so continuous and such considerable change. How is this? Because the wisdom of your forefathers placed the prize of supreme power without the sphere of human passions. Whatever the struggles of parties, whatever the strife of factions, whatever the excitement and exaltation of the public mind, there has always been something in this country round which all classes and parties could rally, representing the majesty of the law, the administration of justice, and involving at the same time, the security for every man's rights and the fountain of honour. Now, gentlemen, it is well clearly to comprehend what it meant by a country not having a revolution for two centuries. It means, for that space, the unbroken exercise and enjoyment of the ingenuity of man. It means the accumulation of capital, the elevation of labour, the establishment of those admirable factories which cover your district; the unwearied improvements of the cultivation of the land, which has extracted from a somewhat churlish soil harvests more exuberant than those furnished by lands nearer to the sun. It means the continuous order which is the only parent of personal liberty and political right."

Winston Churchill

Born in 1874 Churchill had his first major Parliamentary post in 1911 when he was appointed First Lord of the Admiralty. During his stormy political years, in and out of government office, Churchill made many fine speeches, but it is those he delivered as the country's war leader which will endure. There are a number of quotations from them which are now part of public history. Sometimes, as with 'The Few', he deals with a particular subject or group of people. But the pinnacle of his oratory is where he addresses general principles. The peroration of his speech on 'The Battle of Britain' is a classic example:

> "The battle of Britain is about to begin. On this battle depends the survival of Christian civilisation. Upon it depends our own British way of life and the long continuity of our institutions and our empire. The whole fury and might of the enemy must very soon be turned upon us. Hitler knows he will have to break us on this island or lose the war. If we can stand up to him all Europe may be freed and the life of the world may move forward into broad sunlit uplands; but if we fail, the whole world, including the United States, and all that we have known and cared for, will sink into the abyss of a new dark age made more sinister and perhaps more prolonged by the lights of a perverted science. Let us therefore brace ourselves to our duty and so bear ourselves that if the British Commonwealth and Empire last for a thousand years, men will still say this was their finest hour."

There is a remarkable similarity between the speeches of the ancient Greek orators and those of the outstanding statesmen of our own recent history. They flow in a simple, undeviating line from beginning to the final peroration. There is no hyperbole, no deliberate 'purple' passages full of colourful adjectives. The most uneducated could readily understand them and respond to their dramatic message. To achieve that apparent simplicity those orators had to be, and were, outstanding exponents of the spoken word.

The aspiring speaker should intently study their carefully constructed phraseology, and see how it can be used to modify their own efforts. Quote aloud the speech extracts given above. Try to achieve the same dramatic quality of voice – usually grave and without histrionics - with which they were originally delivered. The speaker who can achieve a similar effect will be among the best of his own time.

Mind And Voice In Harmony

"If it is desired that a person shall speak correctly, it is even more desirable that he should think correctly." Ballard wrote that many years ago. A E Mander went further: "People with untrained minds should no more expect to think logically and clearly than people who have never practised should expect to find themselves good golfers ...or pianists." The views of Ballard and Mander emphasise the central theme of this book: perfect diction, tonal quality of voice, breathing control and poise before an audience are essential for the best orators but do not, by themselves, make one.

The quality of your mind, the thoughts you express, will most impress your individuality on an audience and gain its support. It is no coincidence that the most famous orators throughout history have been seekers of wisdom about society and the human condition, and whose mental discipline enabled them to convey their views with mind and voice in perfect harmony. This supreme quality for a public speaker is also the most difficult to achieve, for training the mind takes longer and is more onerous than learning to speak competently. This is perhaps why many able public speakers seem unwilling to take that final step and give the time and mental application necessary.

This chapter cannot teach all the elements of basic philosophical thought, logical reasoning or correct word usage, it can only emphasise the necessity for such study for those who want to achieve excellence. Nevertheless there are certain primary rules which, though not difficult to grasp, help towards the ultimate objective of a trained mind. Those briefly outlined in this chapter should be studied until they become part of an automatic mental filtering process, enabling you to discern fact from fiction, to clarify ambiguity, and to efficiently pursue the main question being discussed until it is resolved.

The Facts

A satisfactory conclusion to any discussion or debate can be reached only on the basis of relevant fact. This was emphasised in the earlier Chapter 8 on 'Debating to Win.' A fact - the known truth of any matter - may be proved scientifically, by continued observation, and by deduction. If, for example, it is constantly demonstrated that two and two always add up to four then that is the fact. It cannot also be a fact that two and two sometimes make five. Nor can it be a fact that all Scotsmen are mean, or all Irishmen are glib, if the existence can be proved of a generous Scotsman or a taciturn Irishman.

Facts which have been proved scientifically by checked observation or methodical research are almost certain to remain constant. But those based on deduction, custom, or general acceptance can change – often fairly drastically – when developments in society, technology or better analytical procedures prove them to be wrong. Throughout history there are numerous examples of this. Many of the facts we now accept about our planet Earth and the universe, and regard them as immutable, were previously held to be false or, worse, grave heresy. Torture and death were the 'debating techniques' used against those who challenged accepted 'wisdom.'

Two thousand five hundred years ago Greek philosophers declared as fact, and it was so accepted, that the earth was a flat disk covered by the dome of the sky. Four hundred years later Eratosthenes deduced by reasoning that the earth was spherical. Then, in the early 17th century, Galileo developed the astronomical telescope to search the sky and not only concluded that Eratosthenes was right but added that the Earth was not the centre of the universe, that it revolved round the sun and was a fairly unimportant part of the universe.

He was treated as a dangerous heretic for his facts, proven by careful observation, were completely contrary to those as declared by the Catholic church over the centuries. Galileo was tried before the Inquisition and finally recanted after being shown the instruments of torture that awaited him if he clung to his 'false' beliefs. But his facts have now been confirmed by even more powerful telescopes, by general observation over the years, and finally by photographs taken from manned space flight.

Less than twenty years after Galileo faced the Inquisition it was widely held as fact that the Earth was only 5,600 years old.

This was based on deduction by Archbishop James Usher of Armagh in Ireland who appeared to have formed his theory after a study of Genesis, the first Book of Moses in the Bible. But we now accept as fact, from all the known scientific evidence, that the Earth is about 4,500 million years old; that it is global in shape; that it rotates; and is not at the centre of the universe.

The lesson is that when faced with a claimed 'fact', unsupported by scientific or other observation, we must train our mental processes to test it against all other related information known to us. It is certainly necessary to be on guard where it amounts to no more than subjective generalisation. "I know most people will agree with me when I say ..." or "I'm sure that a majority of the people would ..." These claims are usually advanced without a scrap of statistical evidence to support them. They are simply superficial assumptions and should be dismissed as such.

Another common error is misunderstanding the relationship of fact to theory, regarding theory as if it were merely unsubstantiated speculation. In Parliament even government ministers are guilty of this. They dismiss an opponent's views by airily declaiming that: "The Hon. Gentleman's theory is quite perfect – except for the slight difficulty that in practice it would also prove quite impossible." When a speaker makes a statement like this he is not being smart but displaying his ignorance. Theories are founded on fact. If a theory is *perfect* then it must work in practice. If it does not then it was imperfect; the final deduction from the basic facts was wrong.

The right word

No two words mean the same. However slight the distinction, one word is more appropriate than another in a given context. To give definitive expression to thought, the correct usage of words is important. It is therefore a bad example to budding orators that highly paid TV broadcasters are so sloppy in their use of the English language, and apparently with the acceptance of the BBC and other station chiefs.

If no two words are precisely the same how can news broadcasters reconcile the use, for example, of the word 'agenda' to mean 'programme, priority, objective, or ambition' when the correct definition is a formal list of subjects to be discussed at a meeting?

"Five or six synonyms may correspond almost exactly, but there is always some little shade of meaning or detail of use that separates them. It is because we forget this so often that our speech becomes full of halting substitutes or long circumlocution's," wrote G H Vallins in his book *Good English*.

Clear thought is difficult to achieve so it deserves clear expression with no ambiguous or woolly use of words that could mislead. It was said that Aneuran Bevan, one of the greatest Parliamentary orators of his generation, had such superb use of language because he frequently browsed through the Oxford dictionary and so gradually acquired his extensive vocabulary. On one notable occasion he accused one speaker of trying to 'denigrate' another. Most people, including the Parliamentary reporters, had never heard of the word and rushed to their dictionaries. They found it was a very precise use of the definition to 'defame'. After that it became commonplace – almost a cliché in itself.

Bevan's use of language was so defined as to be clinical, wielded with the same precision as a surgeon wields a scalpel. The embryonic orator may not reach that stage, or become the fount of newly minted forms of expression, but perfection lies in that direction. Apart from a study of books on English, like the one by Vallins, the Oxford dictionary and Roget's Thesaurus are invaluable for giving definitions of the use of language.

The point in question

Failure to keep to the point under discussion is a certain sign of the untrained mind. Sometimes it is even incapable of clearly seeing the relevant point. Consequently the argument ranges far from its origins and drifts aimlessly without hope of ever reaching a positive conclusion. Whenever the untrained mind faces defeat on an untenable proposition, it quickly attempts to divert to another. Constructive thought is beyond those with a butterfly mentality that flutters randomly about the point but never settles on it. The trained mind will refuse to follow its flight.

Frequently two people involved in debate may believe they are discussing the same point but each is actually thinking of a different aspect of it. The argument is therefore futile and, ultimately, the conclusion may be acrimonious with nothing constructive being resolved - they might as well be talking in different languages. A trained thinker will be able to clearly state the point at issue and seek to get his opponent to agree it. Only then can they move on to a positive discussion.

What do you mean by?

Another short route to acrimony; a debate without first agreeing an exact definition of the subject at issue. Take, for example, the debating title: 'Democracy has been proved down the ages to be the best form of government.' It might be thought unnecessary to first agree on the definition of democracy ("Surely everybody knows what it means!"), so the participants take up their positions on the assumption that it means the same thing to each of them and to all people.

But democracy as a concept has significantly changed down the ages. Is it that every citizen over a certain age has the right to vote at elections? That applied in the old Soviet Union, but only for a single, approved and restricted list of candidates. Is it then that every citizen not only has the right to vote but to stand as a candidate? The old Greek city states have been held by some to be the most effective democracies of their time, but they very narrowly defined the qualifications for being regarded as a 'citizen.' Their economies and prosperity were founded on huge numbers of slaves, like that of the Roman empire, with neither freedom nor votes so the relatively small minority of 'citizens' ruled the great majority.

Even in Britain the franchise was given to women only this century. Britain also dominated a vast empire with great numbers of subservient peoples who had no electoral rights over their destiny. So what exactly do we mean by democracy? The norm now accepted is that all adults have free speech; the right to stand for election and to vote, and there are no slaves or desires for empire.

Only after this definition is agreed by the participating parties is it possible to move on to debate the motion about democracy being better for mankind.

Then again - better for whom? Certainly not for dictators and their henchmen such as we have seen emerging in too many countries throughout the world. And is it better for minorities that all issues be resolved by a majority vote in 'first past the post' local or national government elections, or should there be proportional representation?

It might seem as if the debate will never begin, awaiting definitive answers to the questions raised. But unless the subject is narrowly defined it could be completely fruitless to start. The trained mind will insist that, before a debate begins, its parameters should be clearly agreed to the satisfaction of those taking part.

Never argue with a deity

Whether it be God, Allah, Brahma or some other religion, they are all founded on faith, the opposite of fact. So if your opponent in a debate claims that his argument is justified because of God's will, or that the 'facts' are in the Bible, you should insist that the debate can only take place on facts that are generally accepted, available to both of you, and not founded simply on creed. There can be no constructive conclusion between a person arguing on the basis of fact and one who simply cites religious faith as justification for his views. This is question begging with a vengeance.

The difficulty is not simply one that arises when the debate is between a Christian, Muslim, Buddhist or whatever and a non-believer. The fallacy of arguing on grounds of religion is even more clearly seen when it is between people professing the same faith. History has witnessed conflicts over religion sometimes resulting in war or its limited expression - terrorism. Yet the warring parties may each be Christian, claiming that 'God is on their side' and will help them to victory.

Possibly of greater danger to rational discussion is faith in the infallibility of people who are or were unquestionably alive. The *Mein Kampf* of Adolf Hitler, and the *Little Red Book* of the sayings of Mao Tse Tung were elevated to - and even beyond - the status of the Bible by their supporters. No argument about fascism or communism was possible with those who clung to them as if they were religious beliefs, founded on the word of those regarded as god-like.

The *Das Kapital* of Karl Marx was another bible to the European communists who strictly followed his ideals. No reasonable discussion could take place with a person who answered demands for factual confirmation by repetitively stating that "Karl Marx said ..." The trained mind will not be drawn into this futile kind of discussion.

Colourful Words

These are words, usually adjectival, which reveal a speaker's subjectivity rather than objectivity and you should be on your guard against them. Words like 'good' or 'bad' might indicate a quality that a thing truly possesses; on the other hand they may simply expose a personal prejudice. Historians and governments are very prone to this kind of biased comment. Think of the possible propaganda view by two nations which have been at war and in which one side won a definite victory over the other. The history books and government spokesmen of the opposing sides will use very different terms to describe the defeat. The losers are almost certain to be described thus by their leading orators (spot the colourful adjectives!):

> "The gallant forces of our countrymen, though greatly outnumbered by the massed ranks of a brutal enemy, fought courageously until, against all odds, it looked as if victory might reward their indomitable efforts. But the vast numbers of the enemy, and their much superior weaponry, deprived our forces of the victory their courage so richly deserved. When finally forced to quit the battlefield they did so in an orderly manner, without despondency, and conducted themselves with a pride and dignity which we, their countrymen, share in honour of their great valour."

Of course the victors will not see it quite like that. They will describe an evenly matched battle in which their own gallant forces eventually triumphed over a deceitful, vain, and most experienced enemy, routing them from the battlefield in total and fearful disarray.

It is not only public orators and formal histories that are prejudiced by the use of colourful terminology. In everyday conversation such adjectives will be frequently slipped into discussion. One person may be described by a friend as being 'reserved'; the less enchanted will prefer the term 'cold-blooded'. What one finds as 'warm-hearted', the other will sneer at as 'maudlin sentiment'. A 'staunch conservative' becomes, in the eye of an opponent, a 'bigoted Tory'. A 'loyal labour party member' becomes, for another, a 'crypto-communist stooge'.

By using coloured expressions a person attempts to establish prejudgement without giving supporting evidence. Take the political examples mentioned above. The known fact is that a person is a member of the Conservative Party or the Labour Party. To further define that he is bigoted, or a crypto-communist, there must be a discussion in which the contestants must produce factual evidence in support of their contention. But the casual insertion of the coloured adjective tries to circumvent this discussion and claim that something is true without offering any proofs in support.

The last word

By fully understanding the few rules above, and constantly putting them into practice, you will have considerable advantage over an untrained mind. A more extensive study of philosophy and logical theory will further strengthen your mental armoury and make you a better speaker and very doughty debating opponent. Wide general reading is also essential. We earlier gave a few examples of 'democracy' as it was practised through the ages, and how the enlightened mind would have been able to quote Greek, Roman and early British history. This information you can only get through extensive reading; a trained logical mind and definitive use of language will then enable you to incisively express the benefits of your learning.

The last word? Sir William Drummond once said that: 'He who cannot reason is a fool; he who will not is a bigot; he who dares not is a slave.'